Give Me Five! ENGLISH

PUPIL'S BOOK 6

macmillan education

Donna Shaw • Rob Sved

Syllabus

	Vocabulary	Grammar	Pronunciation
S A new project	Things I see in a town or city Countries and languages	*Are there any (statues in our town)?* *Yes, there are (a few statues in our town).*	
1 Travel trouble	Air travel Travel and tourism	*While I was (taking photos), he (agreed to sign a football).* *I enjoyed (reading about Bertrand Piccard).* *He promised to (make his plane faster).*	Past simple endings: /d/, /ɪd/, /t/
2 Sports and hobbies	Sports and equipment Hobbies	*Have you ever (played tennis)?* *When did they (go sailing)? They (went sailing a month ago).* *How long has he (studied French)? He's (studied French) since (last year).*	Rhythm and stress patterns in present perfect sentences
3 Healthy habits	Food Keeping fit and healthy	*There are too many / aren't enough (tomatoes).* *There's too much / isn't enough (rain at this time of year).* *We should / must / need to (make a cake).* *You shouldn't / mustn't / needn't (stop eating sugar completely).*	Contracted forms: *shouldn't, needn't, mustn't*
Project 1: An energy proposal	An energy proposal	*One advantage of solar energy is that when the sun is shining, there is energy.* *One disadvantage of solar energy is that solar cells are expensive.*	
4 Creative kids	Creative activities Artistic professions	*The (puppet) was / wasn't (made last week).* *When was (the picture painted)?* *Who were (the songs sung) by?*	Words with the silent letter 'w'
5 Write it down!	Messages and communication News features	*He said he (was happy with the results).* *She told me they (weren't very good at tennis).* *He told me it would (rain tomorrow).* *She said they could (read Arabic).*	Sentences with *would* and *could*
6 Our future	Jobs Life events	*I will definitely be (an archaeologist).* *I probably won't be (a politician).* *Do you think you'll be (famous in ten years' time)?*	Rising and falling intonation patterns with modal verbs of possibility and certainty
Project 2: Living on Mars	Conditions for life on Earth and Mars	*What are the things that allow us to live on Earth?* *We need oxygen to breathe. Plants make oxygen, so we need lots of plants.* *We could bring the water from other planets.*	
7 Buying and selling	Money and shopping Describing damaged objects	*I'm too (old) to (play with teddies).* *He isn't (old) enough to (buy a mobile phone).* *(My sister) isn't as (tall) as (her friends).* *If I (finish my homework early), I'll (play computer games).* *What will you do if you (miss the bus this afternoon)?*	Features of connected speech: linking words
8 Let's dream	Activities on a tropical island Unreal or unlikely experiences	*If I (lived in the Galapagos Islands), I would / wouldn't (climb a volcano).* *Would you (take water) if you (abandoned a boat)?* *What would you do if you (were lost at sea)?*	Contracted forms: *would*
9 School: past and future	School equipment Secondary school	*I used to / didn't use to (play computer games).* *Did we use to (have the Internet)?* *I'm going to (have lunch at two o'clock).* *I think he'll (pass the exam).*	Features of connected speech: weak form of *going to*
Project 3: Life in the past	Different aspects of life in the past	*I've got a question about school: What did classrooms look like?* *I'm not sure. That's similar to my question: How did people go to school?*	
Festivals	Thanksgiving Day	Endangered Species Day	

She usually (plays tennis on Saturday morning). Today (she's waiting to have a ride in the hot-air balloon).	*The children live in a big city, don't they?*

Culture	Literacy	21st Century Skills	Cross-curricular links
A solar-powered plane that landed in Belgium	An eyewitness account	**Ways of thinking:** presenting balanced opinions and views	**Science:** Using a compass **Arts and Crafts:** Proportion in portraits
Kung fu and Shaolin monks in China	A magazine article	**Living in the world:** achieving goals	**Science:** First aid techniques **Arts and Crafts:** Representing movement
Story: The discovery of chocolate in Mexico	An argument text	**Ways of working:** recording information and setting routines	**Science:** Nutrition **Arts and Crafts:** Scale and space
Let's propose (solar energy) for the community. *We've got (lots of sun here all year).* *We could put (wind turbines by the coast).*		Preparing a digital presentation about renewable energy in groups	**Science:** Renewable energy **Arts and Crafts:** Baroque art
Japanese manga and anime	A comic strip	**Digital skills:** using digital media creatively	**Science:** Goya **Arts and Crafts:** Expressive lines and colours
Discovering the Rosetta Stone and the meaning of Egyptian hieroglyphics	A newspaper article	**Digital skills:** using digital media to research and present information	**Science:** Information and Communication Technology **Arts and Crafts:** Contour lines
Story: The story of Evelyn Glennie, the Scottish musician	An informal letter	**Ways of thinking:** thinking in different ways	**Science:** EU single market **Arts and Crafts:** Perspective
Let's grow (fruit) here. *We would wear (spacesuits).* *We would travel in (special cars).*		Designing a home on Mars in groups	**Science:** Future technology **Arts and Crafts:** Modern art
How fair trade started in the USA	An advert	**Living in the world:** initiative and entrepreneurial skills	**Science:** The Eurozone **Arts and Crafts:** Depth in landscapes
How a couple were lost at sea for 117 days near the Galapagos Islands	A diary extract	**Ways of working:** working as a team	**Science:** Physical geography of Spain and Europe **Arts and Crafts:** Analogous colours
Story: The creation of the Nobel Prizes in Sweden	An advice column	**Living in the world:** managing strong feelings	**Science:** Virtual museum: past and present **Arts and Crafts:** Volume
What did she say about (life at school)? *She said she (sat at the same desk every day).*		Presenting information gathered on life in the past	**Science:** Life in the 20th century **Arts and Crafts:** Art today

Cambridge Exams Practice Practice for B1 Preliminary for Schools: Reading and Writing (see page 124 for Syllabus)

Starter Unit A new project

Objectives In this unit, I will ...

- name things I see in a town or city.
- listen to descriptions and identify people.
- use question tags.
- learn about global e-projects.

1 Look at the photo and read. Answer the questions. Whole Class

1 What can you see in the photo?
2 What are the people going to do?
3 Have you ever had a ride in a hot-air balloon?
4 Would you like to have a ride in a hot-air balloon? Why? / Why not?

2 Communicate Read about the hot-air balloon rides. Answer the questions.

1 When can you have a hot-air balloon ride?
2 How long does the ride last?
3 Can children ride alone?
4 Which animals will people help if they have a hot-air balloon ride?

3 How old are Tom, Jess and Callum? Listen and read. Act out. CD1 1

4 Which six things do the children see during the hot-air balloon ride? Listen and find out. CD1 2

statue skate park bridge block of flats stadium department store tunnel factory square cycle path

5 Communicate Ask and answer questions about where you live.

Are there any statues in our town?

Yes, there are a few statues in our town.

1 **Read and identify the person in the queue.**

Emma usually **plays** tennis on Saturday morning, but today she**'s waiting** in the queue to have a ride in the hot-air balloon. She **likes** photography so she**'s carrying** a camera. She **wants** to take lots of photos when she's in the air. Can you see her?

2 **Listen and identify other people in the queue.** CD1 3

3 **Read and answer these questions about Activity 1.** Whole Class

1 What's Emma's routine on Saturday morning? Do we use the present simple or the present continuous to talk about routines?

2 What's Emma doing now? Do we use the present simple or the present continuous to talk about things that are happening now?

3 Do we use the verbs *want* and *like* in the present simple, present continuous or both?

4 **Thinking skills Look at the verbs. Which ones can only be used in the present simple? Which ones can be used in the present simple and the present continuous?**

~~dislike~~ climb work understand believe swim know want prefer eat travel go

Only present simple	Present simple and present continuous
dislike	

5 **Communicate Ask and answer the questions. Then think of another question to ask your partner.**

1 Which activities do you dislike doing? Why?

2 Do you prefer taking photos or making videos? Why?

3 Do you think hot-air balloons are dangerous? Why? / Why not?

4 What do you want to do this weekend? Why?

1 Listen and read. Answer the questions.

CD1 4

Mr Owen: What did you do at the weekend, Jess?

Jess: I had a hot-air balloon ride in the park.

Mr Owen: Really? Was there a special reason for the ride?

Jess: Yes, the money from the hot-air balloon rides is going to be used to protect wild birds.

Tom: It's a great project. We'd like to find out how other people help in their communities.

Mr Owen: I know about a global project called 'Make a difference'. Schoolchildren from different countries write and share their ideas about helping in the community. Their logo is a hot-air balloon. Why don't you join?

Callum: It sounds amazing! And we can learn about life in other countries, too.

1 Who was in the park at the weekend?
2 Why was the hot-air balloon ride a good idea?
3 What's the global project called?
4 What can you do if you join the project?

2 Quickly read about the schools in the *Make a difference* project. How many schools are in Europe? Where are the other schools?

Make a difference

Welcome to the *Make a difference* project!

Make a difference

Do you know that there are schools around the world that are helping their local communities? Here's a list of the exciting projects organised by schools participating in the *Make a difference* project:

Project: Posters for passengers
Country: Belgium
Official languages: French, Dutch, German

Project: Sport for everyone
Country: China
Official language: Chinese

Project: A community garden
Country: Mexico
Official language: Spanish

Project: Theatre fun
Country: Japan
Official language: Japanese

Project: Reading is cool!
Country: Egypt
Official language: Arabic

Project: A helping hand
Country: Scotland
Official languages: English, Gaelic, Scots

Project: An 'almost new' sale
Country: the USA
Official language: English

Project: Let's clean up!
Country: Ecuador
Official language: Spanish

Project: Computer lessons
Country: Sweden
Official language: Swedish

Why don't you join our project and tell us how you're making a difference in your community? You can practise your English, too. To join, your class teacher must complete the online form at register@makeadifference.com

3 Communicate Play a memory game in pairs. Ask and answer.

Which languages are spoken in Scotland?

English, Gaelic and Scots are spoken there.

Key learning outcomes: listen to and answer questions about helping communities; review countries and languages spoken there; ask and answer questions about languages

1 **Look at the photos. What do you think the children have written about their *Make a difference* project?** Whole Class

2 **Read and find out.**

Make a difference

HOME NEWS BLOG CONTACT US SEARCH

PROJECT: THE BALLOON PROJECT
COUNTRY: ENGLAND

Hi, everyone!

We're really happy to be part of the 'Make a difference' project. We live in a town in the south-east of England. It's in the middle of beautiful countryside. Unfortunately, some species of birds are in danger. This is because there are fewer places for them to build nests and there are more predators like foxes, cats and dogs.

Last weekend, we paid some money to go up in a hot-air balloon and experience what it's like to be a bird. Here's a photo of what we could see from the air. It was amazing!

The money from the hot-air balloon ride will pay for some nest boxes for birds. These boxes provide a safe place for them to lay eggs. Here's a photo of a nest box for barn owls. It's really cool, isn't it?

We want to raise more money for nest boxes and hear about what you do to make a difference in your community. Please write and tell us.

Jess, Callum and Tom

3 **Read and think. Choose.**

Think about grammar

Question tags

Negative question tag:
The children live in a big town, don't they?

Positive question tag:
Cats aren't predators, are they?

1 When the sentence is **affirmative**, the question tag is *negative / positive.*
2 When the sentence is **negative**, the question tag is *negative / positive.*

4 **Look at the text in Activity 2 again. Find an example of a question tag.**

5 **Communicate Ask and answer.**

You've got three brothers and sisters, haven't you?

No, I haven't. I've got one brother and one sister.

1 You've got ? brothers and sisters, haven't you?
2 You enjoy playing ? , don't you?
3 You can't ? , can you?
4 Your favourite food is ? , isn't it?
5 You don't like ? , do you?
6 You're feeling ? , aren't you?

Remember!
- I'm not 12, am I?
- I'm 11, aren't I?

Key learning outcomes: read and understand an information text about a balloon project in England; use question tags to check information

Unit 1 Travel trouble

Objectives **In this unit, I will ...**

- name things associated with air travel.
- make sentences using *while* and the past continuous.
- learn about Belgium and about Solar Impulse, a solar-powered plane.
- learn to use verbs that are followed by an infinitive or a gerund.
- read and write an eyewitness account of a historical event.
- have a conversation about travel.
- learn how to present a balanced opinion and view.

Look! A school in Belgium has left a message on the project's website. I wonder how the children there make a difference.

Make a difference

Hi, everyone! My name's Julie. Our local airport is organising an exhibition. **They've asked people in our community to make posters, including our school.** I love travelling and I find going to the airport really exciting. But many people have to travel for work and are away from their families. Hopefully the posters will cheer them up! A group of us are visiting the airport tomorrow to get ideas for our poster. Then we have to decide what to do. We've had a look at some photos, too. Should we do the poster about life at an airport?

1

2

3

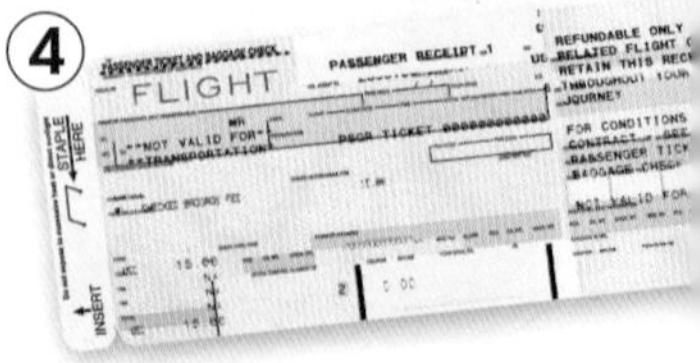

4

5

6

7

8

1 Look at the photos Julie has sent. Answer the questions. Whole Class

1 What can you see in the photos?
2 Have you ever been to an airport?
3 If so, why did you go there?

2 Look and match with photos 1–12. Listen, check and repeat. CD1 5

departures arrivals boarding pass land check-in desk queue trolley take off passenger flight attendant runway hand luggage

3 Listen and do the vocabulary quiz. CD1 6

4 Thinking skills Think about travelling. Copy the chart. Complete it with things you put in your hand luggage and things you put in your suitcase.

In my hand luggage	In my suitcase
passport	socks

Key learning outcomes: identify and name things associated with air travel; talk about ideas presented in posters
Vocabulary: air travel

5 **Thinking skills** **Read the rest of Julie's message. Which poster idea do you think is the best?**

We shared some ideas for our poster at school today. Now we have to choose the best one. We need to think about what would make people happy, and what would be fun for people to look at. What do you think?

An airport can be the start of an adventure. This idea for a poster shows famous places in the world, such as the Pyramids in Egypt, the Eiffel Tower in Paris and Mount Everest.

One group suggested showing the different people who work at an airport. It would also have some interesting facts. Did you know that more than 20,000 planes take off in the USA every day?

Airports are full of people of all nationalities. One group suggested a poster that shows children from around the world holding hands. They're saying 'hello' in their languages.

6 **Communicate** **Ask and answer about the posters.**

Which poster idea would you choose?

I'd choose the one about the different nationalities.

Why?

Because it's got a positive and optimistic message and it would make people feel happy.

1 **Describe the photo. Why do you think Julie talks about this team? Read and listen to find out.** CD1 7

Hi, Julie. Your project is brilliant. Have you decided which poster to do yet?

Thanks, Jess. No, not yet.

Did you enjoy your trip to the airport?

Yes, we did. It was really interesting. And it gave us lots of ideas.

That's great.

And guess what? While we were walking around the airport, we saw a player from the Belgian football team!

Lucky you!

And while I was taking photos, he agreed to sign a football and bring it to our school!

Brilliant! Will you post photos when you've got the ball?

Of course. While I was at the airport, I discovered something else, too. I learnt about a solar-powered plane that landed here in Belgium. I'll send you some information about it.

A solar-powered plane? That sounds interesting.

2 **Communicate Read the dialogue again. Which sentence is true?**

1 Julie saw the football player before she walked around the airport.
2 Julie saw the football player after she walked around the airport.
3 Julie saw the football player at the same time as she was walking around the airport.

3 **Look and learn.**

Grammar Wall

Past simple & past continuous with *while*

While I was taking photos, he agreed to sign a football.

I saw a hot-air balloon while I was walking to school.

4 **Read and think. Choose.**

Think about grammar

1 We use the *past simple / past continuous* for the short action.
2 We use the *past simple / past continuous* with **while** for the longer action that is interrupted.

5 **Look at the dialogue in Activity 1 again. Find more examples of the past simple and the past continuous being used together.**

6 **Communicate Invent things that could interrupt these actions. Ask and answer.**

1 

What happened while you were sleeping on the beach?

While I was sleeping on the beach, a crab bit my toe!

2 

3 

4 

Key learning outcomes: use the past simple and the past continuous to describe actions that were interrupted
Grammar: simple past and past continuous

Before you read

1 **Thinking skills** Whole Class

Read and discuss.

- What can you see in the photo on the right?
- What are they used for?
- Do you think they're important for the future? Why? / Why not?
- How could they be used for travel?

2 **Listen and read.** CD1 9

Flying

A PLANE THAT COULD FLY FOREVER!

Flying without fuel

After his balloon flight in 1999, Bertrand Piccard promised to fly around the world without using any fuel. He started building a plane that only used energy from the sun. The plane had to be very light and needed long wings covered with solar panels. It took many years to build this new plane. He called the plane Solar Impulse.

The record-breaking flight

In May 2011, the plane was ready to fly from Switzerland to Belgium, its first international flight. André Borschberg, Piccard's colleague, was the pilot. While Borschberg was flying the plane, Piccard's team and a large crowd of people arrived at Brussels Airport. It was a long, nervous wait. After 13 hours, the plane came into sight. While it was moving towards the runway, the weather became windy and Borschberg had to turn the plane around. They decided to use a different runway and the plane landed safely. Crowds of people cheered.

Name: Bertrand Piccard **Born:** 1958

Explorers in the family: his grandfather was a balloonist and his father was an undersea explorer.

First famous achievement: he flew around the world in a hot-air balloon without stopping.

A fuel-free future?

Piccard's plane took off from Switzerland with little energy in the batteries. During the flight, the batteries were charging. The plane landed with more energy than when it took off! In 2016, Piccard flew the Solar Impulse 2, and completed the first round-the-world flight. The journey took 505 days, but only used solar power. Can you imagine flying without fuel in the future?

After you read

Go to page 8 in your Activity Book.

Values

- **Why is Bertrand Piccard's project important for the future of our planet?**
- **What do you do to help save the planet's energy?**
- **What changes could we make to the way we live to save more energy?**

Key learning outcomes: read a story with a cultural focus about solar energy; listen for specific information
Values: the importance of saving the planet's energy

1 Listen and read. Act out. CD1 11

Jess: I enjoyed reading about Bertrand Piccard.

Tom: It's amazing that a plane can fly without any fuel.

Jess: Yes. Piccard suggested using the technology for other forms of transport, too.

Tom: Really? But the plane goes very slowly.

Jess: That's true, but Piccard promised to make his plane faster next time.

Tom: Did you know that our school is going to use solar energy, too?

Jess: Really?

Tom: Yes. They've agreed to put solar panels on the school roof to save energy.

2 Look and learn.

Grammar Wall

Verbs that are followed by the infinitive or the gerund

I enjoyed **reading** about Bertrand Piccard.

Piccard promised **to make** his plane faster next time.

3 Read and think. Choose.

Think about grammar

1 Some verbs, such as **enjoy**, are followed by *an infinitive / a gerund.*

2 Other verbs, such as **promise**, are followed by *an infinitive / a gerund.*

You will need to remember which verbs use a gerund and which verbs use an infinitive.

4 Look at the article on page 11 and the dialogue in Activity 1 again. Are these verbs followed by an infinitive or a gerund?

agree   suggest   imagine   decide   start

5 Read and listen to the different verb endings. Put the verbs in the correct column. CD1 12

Pronunciation

imagined   decided   started
stopped   agreed   liked   tried

/d/	/ɪd/	/t/
enjoyed	suggested	promised

6 Add more verbs to each column in Activity 5. Check with a partner.

7 Communicate Complete these sentences. Ask and answer.

This month, I started …   This year, I promised …
This morning, I decided …   Today, I enjoyed …
While working in a group this week, I tried …

This month, I started doing my homework at the weekend. How about you?

This month, I started playing tennis every week.

Key learning outcomes: identify and practise past simple endings; use the gerund and infinitive appropriately
Grammar: infinitives and gerunds

1 Look and match. Listen, check and repeat. CD1 14

receptionist guest backpacker ticket office guard
tourist information centre platform reception lift

2 Listen and say *A*, *B* or *C*. CD1 15

Listening tip!
Look carefully at the picture before you listen. Where are the people?

1 Where did Amy's family leave the passports?

2 What was happening at the station?

3 Listen again. Which of these verbs can you hear in the past continuous? CD1 15

play start happen walk want drop

4 Communicate Look at the pictures and remember. Ask and answer.

Teacher's Resource Bank: Unit 1

Can you remember what was happening at the station?

A man was pushing a trolley.

What was on the trolley?

Three suitcases.

Yes, that's right.

Key learning outcomes: identify and use words about travel; listen for specific information; use the past continuous **Vocabulary:** travel nouns

Before you read

1 Read and discuss. Whole Class

- Do you like reading about historical events?
- Have you read any stories that help you learn about historical events? Which ones?
- What do you know about the Titanic?

2 Look at the pictures. Who do you think is telling the story? Read and find out.

Reading tip!
Use the title to make predictions about the text before you read.

The Titanic: first and last voyage

I boarded the Titanic in Southampton on 10th April 1912 with my aunt and uncle. We were going back to New York after staying in England for more than a year. The ship was the most beautiful thing I had ever seen. It was huge and luxurious.

I couldn't believe I was inside a ship floating across the ocean. There was music playing. I saw the captain on the deck, Captain Smith. He had a big white beard and he reached down and shook my hand. He spoke in a deep voice and he promised to show us some of the first-class areas. There was a gymnasium, a swimming pool and many dining rooms.

I was sleeping in our cabin when the Titanic hit the iceberg. There was a sudden jolt and the ship stopped moving. A steward knocked on our door and told us to get dressed, put on our lifejackets and go up to the deck.

The lifts weren't working so we walked up the stairs. An officer was shouting 'women and children first', and people started climbing into lifeboat number 11. Everything was happening so fast. We said a quick goodbye to my uncle and the officers lowered the lifeboat down to the sea. I could hear that the orchestra was still playing.

The lifeboat was swinging from side to side. It was the only time I was scared. While the boats moved away from the ship, we watched the round porthole windows of the ship sink one by one into the calm sea. I was a typical boy of those times. We weren't allowed to cry. I lay down at the bottom of the lifeboat and went to sleep. When I woke up, I saw the huge white icebergs. They looked beautiful, but then I remembered the events of the night before.

After you read

3 What do you think? Whole Class

- This is a fictional story based on real events. Which part of the story is the most interesting?
- What do we learn about the sinking of the Titanic?
- Do you think it's a good thing to write about real events through the eyes of someone who was there? Why? / Why not?

Go to page 11 in your Activity Book.

Key learning outcomes: read an eyewitness report for general understanding; scan a text for specific information; discuss the advantages and disadvantages of an eyewitness report

Text type: **an eyewitness account**

Investigate a text

1 **Look at these headlines. When do you think the events happened? Imagine being there. What would you see, hear and feel? Which of these events is described in Activity 2?** Whole Class

The first hot-air balloon flight | The first man on the moon | Germany win the World Cup

2 **Read the account to find out if you guessed correctly.**

date → It was 21st November 1783.

introduction → Two men were going to fly over Paris in a hot-air balloon for the first time. I was allowed to go with my father and watch it take off.

describing the scene → All the important people in the city were there – the mayor, doctors and lawyers. Women were wearing hats with big feathers. I felt so excited to be there. A huge fire in the square filled the balloon with hot air.

describing using the senses → The smoke smelled terrible and I started coughing. Soon we saw the bright blue and gold balloon, ready for take-off. The two men stood on either end of the balloon basket and the balloon slowly began to rise. Everyone was cheering and clapping as the balloon floated over the park.

reflection → It looked beautiful!

Discuss a text

3 **Read the account again. Answer the questions.** Whole Class

1 Who's writing the account?
2 Why does the writer include a date?
3 Which sentences give an introduction to the event?
4 The writer uses the past continuous to describe the events. Why?
5 Which senses does the writer use?
6 How did the writer feel about seeing the event?

Writing skills: Verbs of the senses

These verbs help describe an experience. They help give personal opinions in eyewitness accounts. We use these verbs with an adjective, or with **like** + a noun:

The costumes ***looked*** *fantastic.*
The ice cream ***tasted*** *delicious.*
The music ***sounded*** *soft and beautiful.*
I ***felt*** *nervous but excited.*
The flowers ***smelled*** *like perfume.*
The hot-air balloon ***looked*** *like a floating ball.*

4 **Look at the two accounts again. Find examples of verbs of the senses.**

➔ **Research, plan and write an eyewitness account of a historical event on page 12 in your Activity Book.**

Key learning outcomes: identify headlines; identify features of an eyewitness report; write an eyewitness report

1 **Look at the photos. What do they show? How are they different?** *Whole Class*

2 **Listen to the conversation. Has Alec ever been abroad?** CD1 17

3 **Listen again. Complete the five questions that Ella asks.** CD1 17

- Have you … ?
- Which is the most … ?
- How … ?
- Are you … ?
- Are you … ?

4 **Prepare a conversation about travel on page 13 in your Activity Book.**

Conversation time

Think about how you can show excitement.

That's so cool!
That's great!
That's fantastic!

Go to the Song Bank, page 125.

5 **Reflect on the unit** **Read and think about your learning. What can you do now?** *Whole Class*

Hi, Julie. Thanks for all your messages. I've learnt so much about your project and about travel.

Thanks, Jess. Good luck with your project, too!

- I can describe actions in the past using *while*.
- I can find Belgium on a map and talk about solar planes.
- I can read and write an eyewitness account.
- I can have a conversation about travel.

Do the Unit Review on page 14 in your Activity Book.

Key learning outcomes: listen to and have a conversation about travel; review learning and reflect on progress in the unit

21 CHANNEL reports

Today's programme is about transport. What transport do you have in your town? How do you go to school?

1 **Watch the video. Read and say *true* or *false*. Correct the false sentences.**

1 Everyone in Max's dad's office walks to work.
2 La Paz, in Bolivia, is a very flat city.
3 The cable car in San Francisco has a cable under the road.
4 Many people can sit in one cycle rickshaw.
5 The monorail in Germany is less than 100 years old.

2 **Match the words to the pictures. Which form of transport does Amy mention in the video?**

motorbikes   cable car   underground   cycle rickshaw   monorail

a

b

c

d

e

3 **Read, think and answer.** Whole Class

Having a balanced view

It is important to be balanced when you are working on a project. Read these tips. Can you think of any more tips?

- For each idea, think of the good things ...
- ... and the bad things.
- Take time to think about your ideas.
- Share opinions.

4 **Work with a partner. Think of good and bad things about each form of transport in your town.** Brainstorm ???

cycle rickshaw   bus   taxi   bicycle

Cycle rickshaws are good for the environment.

Yes, but they only carry one or two people.

Key learning outcomes: watch and understand a video about transport
21st **Ways of thinking:** presenting balanced opinions and views

Unit 2 Sports and hobbies

Objectives In this unit, I will ...

- learn the names of sports and hobbies.
- ask and answer questions about sports and hobbies I've tried.
- learn about China and the history of kung fu.
- talk about how long I've done sports and hobbies.
- read and write a magazine article about a famous person.
- have a conversation about sport.
- learn how to achieve my goals.

Wow! I've just received a message from China. Let's find out how the children make a difference there.

Make a difference

Hi, everyone! My name's Mei and I live in Shanghai, a city on the east coast of China. Last month, my class learnt about a school in the countryside that didn't have any sports equipment, so we decided to help. **We collected old games and toys and sold them at the school fair.** Then we used the money to buy some new sports equipment for the rural school. Here are some photos of the things we bought and some photos of the sports my classmates love doing in their free time. I hope you like them.

1

2

3

4

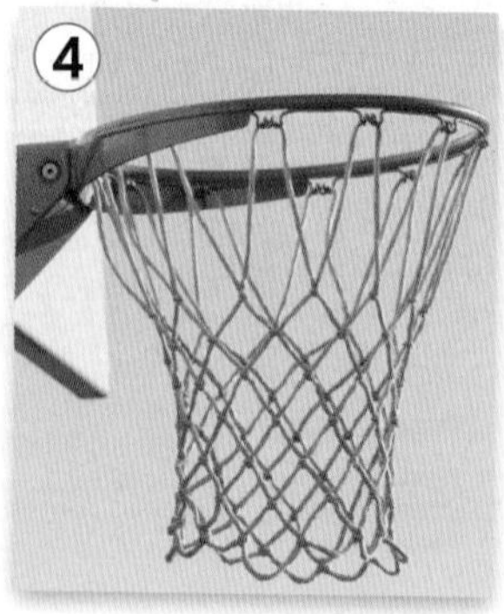

5

7

6

1 Look at Mei's photos. Answer the questions. Whole Class

1 Which sports equipment have you used?
2 What did you do with it?
3 Which sport looks the most fun? Why?
4 Which sports do you enjoy doing?

2 Look and match with photos 1–12. Listen, check and repeat. CD1 19

archery gymnastics fencing athletics
water polo trampolining martial arts
net rope racket hoop crash mat

3 Listen and do the vocabulary quiz. CD1 20

4 Thinking skills How do the words connect?

tennis / badminton fencing / archery hoop / net
water polo / volleyball gymnastics / martial arts

You need a racket to play tennis and badminton.

5 **Thinking skills** **Read the rest of Mei's message. Which fact do you think is untrue?**

My favourite sport is badminton. Here are some amazing facts about this sport. Can you guess which one is untrue?

BADMINTON fun facts

1. Badminton is the fastest racket sport in the world. Some players can hit a ball called a shuttlecock at more than 300km/h.
2. There are more people in the world who play badminton than basketball.
3. The shortest official badminton match in the world lasted only six minutes.
4. A badminton player can run more than 10km on the court in just one match.
5. Badminton is played with a shuttlecock. A shuttlecock has got 16 feathers on it. The best feathers come from the left wing of a goose.
6. In the past, the Chinese played a version of badminton called Ti Zian Ji. However, they didn't use rackets to hit the ball. They used their feet.

Answer: number 4 is untrue. A badminton player can run over 2km in a match.

6 **Communicate** **Ask and answer about sports.**

What equipment do you need to play volleyball?

You need a net and a ball.

What are the rules?

You must pass the ball to your teammates and hit it over the net.

1 Describe the photo. Do you know the name of this activity? Read and listen to find out.

CD1 21

Callum: Hi, Mei. Your project sounds amazing.

Mei: Thanks, Callum. I'm sure the school will be happy with the sports equipment.

Callum: Will the children use the rope for skipping?

Mei: No. They'll use it to play tug-of-war. It's a traditional sport in China. Look!

Callum: That looks great fun. Have you ever played tug-of-war?

Mei: Yes, of course.

Callum: Really? When did you play it?

Mei: I played it at a camp last summer. My team lost, but we didn't mind.

Callum: What other traditional Chinese sports and games have you tried?

Mei: I've played chess and I've done kung fu, too.

Callum: Kung fu! But that's a violent sport, isn't it?

Mei: Not at all. There's some information about kung fu on my class wiki. I'll send it to you.

2 Communicate Read the dialogue again and correct the sentences.

1 Tug-of-war is a modern Chinese sport.
2 Mei played tug-of-war two years ago.
3 Mei has tried five traditional Chinese sports.
4 Mei thinks that kung fu is violent.

3 Look and learn.

Grammar Wall

Present perfect & past simple questions

Present perfect questions

Have	I/you/we/they	ever	played tennis? been sailing? done athletics?
Has	he/she		

Yes, I/you/we/they **have**. Yes, he/she **has**.
No, I/you/we/they **haven't**. No, he/she **hasn't**.

Past simple questions

When	did	I/you/he/she/we/they	play tennis? go sailing? do athletics?

4 Read and think. Choose.

Think about grammar

1 We use the *present perfect* / *past simple* to ask about an experience in the past.
2 We use the *present perfect* / *past simple* to ask more questions about this experience.

5 Look at the dialogue in Activity 1 again. Find more examples of present perfect and past simple questions.

6 Communicate Ask and answer.

go: jogging, horse riding, cycling
play: water polo, volleyball, badminton
do: archery, a martial art, trampolining

Have you ever done archery?
Yes, I have.
When did you do it?
I did it when I was seven.

Key learning outcomes: use the present perfect and past simple to make questions
Grammar: present perfect and past simple questions

Before you read

Mei sent me this information from her class wiki.

1 **Thinking skills** Whole Class

Read and discuss.

- What can you see in the photo on the right?
- What do you know about this sport?
- Do you think it's difficult to do? Why? / Why not?
- Would you like to try it? Why? / Why not?

2 **Listen and read.** CD1 23

Kung fu

KUNG FU

HISTORY

About 1,500 years ago, Chinese monks started using kung fu for self-defence and to protect their temples. The most famous monks lived in the Shaolin Temple where they trained their bodies and minds to help people and to understand the world around them. Nowadays, Shaolin monks travel all around the world to demonstrate their kung fu skills. They have also appeared on television and millions of people have seen their amazing strength and flexibility.

Kung fu

NOUN /ˌkʌŋ ˈfuː/

Kung means skill and *fu* means man. When we put these words together it means skill achieved through hard work.

STYLES

Shaolin monks divide kung fu into five styles which are based on the movements of animals. The most powerful and energetic style is the dragon. The tiger style helps develop strength and the leopard style develops power and speed. The snake style develops flexibility and the crane style develops balance and fast foot movement. All five styles develop discipline and self-control.

TRAINING

Children can begin training with the Shaolin monks when they're about six years old. They get up at five o'clock in the morning to exercise and go to bed at nine o'clock in the evening. Trainee monks aren't allowed to play computer games and their diet is only rice and vegetables. However, they can play football in their free time and they're brilliant players.

After you read

Go to page 18 in your Activity Book.

Values

- What do all five kung fu styles develop?
- Why is it important to have self-control?
- What makes you feel angry?
- How can you control your temper?

Key learning outcomes: read a story with a cultural focus; listen for specific information
Values: the importance of self-control

1 Listen and read. Act out. CD1 25

Callum: Are you interested in martial arts, Tom?
Tom: Yes, I am. I do karate twice a week.
Callum: I didn't know that. Do you like it?
Tom: Yes, it's good fun. I get fit and it helps me concentrate, too.
Callum: How long have you done karate?
Tom: I've done it since I was eight. I've got an orange belt now.
Callum: Really? How long have you had your orange belt?
Tom: I've had it for six months. If I work hard, I'll get a green belt next.
Callum: Can you show me a karate move?
Tom: Yes, of course. Watch this!

2 Look and learn.

Grammar Wall

Present perfect

How long	have	I/you/we/they	played tennis?
	has	he/she	studied French?
I/You/We/They	have	played tennis	for two years.
He/She	has	studied French	since last year.

3 Read and think. Choose.

Think about grammar

1 We use **for** to talk about the period of time.
For: *two days, six months, one year, a long time*
2 We use **since** to say when the action started.
Since: *Friday, last year, 5th November, I was five*
3 We use the present perfect with **for** or **since** when the action *has / hasn't* finished.

4 Look at the article on page 21 and the dialogue in Activity 1 again. Find more examples of the present perfect.

5 Listen and read. Why are some words underlined? Listen again and repeat. CD1 26

Pronunciation

1 How long have you played the piano?
2 I've played the piano for three years.
3 How long have you worn glasses?
4 I've worn glasses since I was six.
5 How long has she lived next door?
6 She's lived next door for a long time.

6 Communicate Ask and answer. Think of more activities.

study English? have a camera?
play football? live in Madrid?
like pop music? do athletics?

Key learning outcomes: practise rhythm and stress patterns in present perfect sentences
Grammar: present perfect

1 Look and match. Listen, check and repeat. CD1 28

sing in a choir do circus skills collect cards belong to a sports club
go to drama class do photography do needlework make models

2 Listen and say *A*, *B* or *C*. CD1 29

Listening tip!
Listen for the general idea first. Focus on the words you know.

1 What does Sophie enjoy collecting?

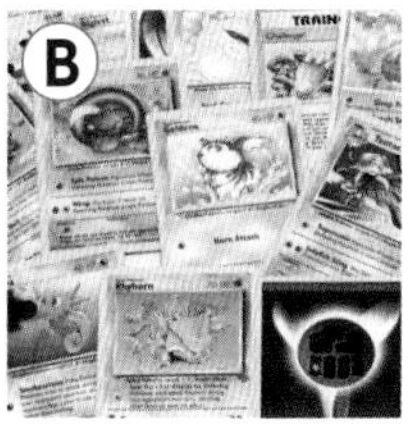

2 What's Sue's hobby?

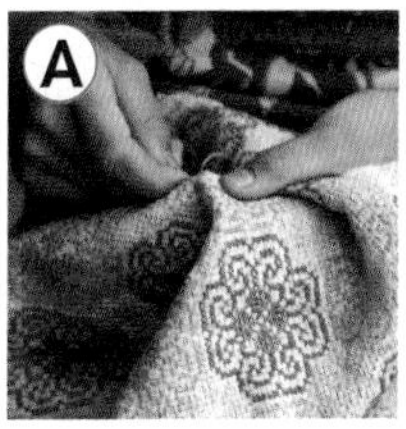

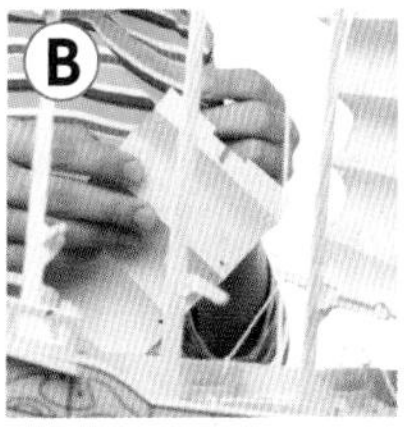

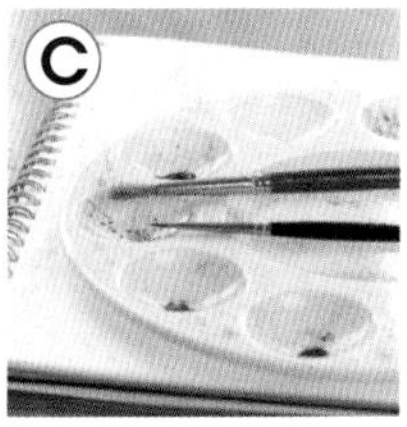

3 Listen again. Which expressions do the children use to say what they prefer? CD1 29

- I prefer collecting stamps to cards.
- I'd rather collect stamps than cards.
- I prefer making models now.
- I'd rather make models now.

4 Communicate Ask and answer to complete the chart.

Teacher's Resource Bank: Unit 2

What does Silvia do in her free time?

How long has she sung in a choir?

She sings in a choir.

She's sung in a choir since she was ten.

Key learning outcomes: identify and say the names of different hobbies; listen for specific information; talk about hobbies **Vocabulary:** hobbies

Literacy

Before you read

1 Read and discuss. Whole Class

- Are you interested in reading about the lives of famous people? Why? / Why not?
- Where can we find out information about them?
- Which famous people have you read about in magazines? What did you find out?

2 Look at the photos. Why do you think this person is famous? Read and find out.

Reading tip!
Look at the pictures before you read. Try and guess what they show.

My favourite sports star

Gisela Pulido is an incredible kitesurfer. She can travel across the waves at more than 40km/h and jump ten metres into the air before landing in the water again.

Gisela was born in Barcelona in 1994 and from a young age she loved sports. She began having kitesurfing lessons when she was eight, and in 2003 she entered the European Junior Championship and won first place in the under-14 category. After that, her family decided to move to Tarifa in the south of Spain so she could combine training with her school work. In the summer holidays, she travelled all around the world to compete in international kitesurfing competitions. When she was only ten, Gisela became the youngest kitesurfing world champion and since then she's been the world champion ten more times.

Gisela is still one of the best kitesurfers in the world.

She's hard-working and self-confident and she loves her sport. She also loves new challenges. She's raced a ferry in the Mediterranean Sea and she's sailed the enormous waves in the south of Australia.

Now, there is a Gisela Pulido kitesurfing school in Tarifa, with a shop that sells great kitesurfing equipment.

I think that Gisela is an amazing sportswoman and I'm sure that she'll win a lot more competitions in the future. You can follow Gisela on many social media sites.

Written by Samantha Owen (aged 14)

After you read

3 What do you think? Whole Class

- Do you think Gisela is an interesting person? Why? / Why not?
- Which information in the article is the most interesting?
- Would you like to find out more information about Gisela? What would you like to know?

Go to page 21 in your Activity Book.

Key learning outcomes: read a magazine article for general understanding; scan an article for specific information; discuss the article's main featured person

Text type: **a magazine article**

Investigate a text

1 **Read the information. Write two open and two closed questions about Ross Lynch.** Whole Class

> It's a good idea to make a list of questions before you research a person.

> Closed questions have got two possible answers: *yes* and *no*. *Does Gisela live in Tarifa?*

> Open questions have got different possible answers. *Why does Gisela live in Tarifa?*

2 **Read the article. Does it answer your questions?**

title → # MY FAVOURITE STAR

Written by Jodie Allen (aged 12)

introduction → Ross Lynch is an American singer, musician, dancer and actor.

biographical facts → He was born in Colorado in 1995 and he started dancing when he was very young. When he was 12, his family moved to California. He learnt how to play the guitar there and he created a band called R5 with two of his brothers, his sister and a friend. Ross also started acting, and when he was 16 he won the part of Austin Moon in the popular television series *Austin and Ally*. Since then, he's appeared in several films and he's recorded some brilliant music CDs. He's won many awards for his acting and music videos.

unusual facts → Ross loves flying and making model planes. He also enjoys drawing and sketching in his free time.

opinion → I think that Ross is a fantastic actor and musician. I'm sure that he'll be a huge star in the future.

photo →

Discuss a text

3 **Read the article again. Answer the questions.** Whole Class

1 What's the title?
2 What do we find out in the introduction?
3 Which facts are in the second paragraph?
4 Which facts are in the third paragraph?
5 What's the writer's opinion?
6 Why is there a photo?

Writing skills: Extreme adjectives

We use extreme adjectives to make texts more exciting and more interesting to read:

good – ***brilliant, fantastic, amazing***
big – ***huge, enormous, massive***
surprising – ***astonishing***
interesting – ***fascinating***

Remember that we can't write **very** before an extreme adjective.

4 **Look at both articles again. Find examples of extreme adjectives.**

➔ **Plan and write a magazine article about a famous person on page 22 in your Activity Book.**

Key learning outcomes: identify and write open and closed questions; identify parts of an article; write a magazine article; use extreme adjectives

1 Describe the photos. Have you ever done these sports? Whole Class

2 Listen to the conversation. Which sport does James talk about? CD1 31

3 Listen again. Complete the four questions that Anna asks. CD1 31

• How often ...? • Do ...? • Who ...? • Would ...?

4 ➔ Prepare a conversation about your favourite sports on page 23 in your Activity Book.

Conversation time

Remember to tell people if it's difficult to understand them.

Sorry, can you speak more loudly, please?

Sorry, can you speak more slowly, please?

5 Reflect on the unit Read and think about your learning. What can you do now? Whole Class

I can talk about how long I've done sports and hobbies.

I can find China on a map and talk about kung fu.

I can read and write a magazine article about a famous person.

I can have a conversation about sport.

➔ Do the Unit Review on page 24 in your Activity Book.

Key learning outcomes: listen to and have a conversation about sport; review learning and reflect on progress in the unit

21 CHANNEL reports

Today's programme is about hobbies. Have you got any hobbies? Are you good at them?

1 Watch the video. Read and answer the questions.

1 How often does Max's brother play the piano?
2 How long has Max's cousin had guitar lessons?
3 What does Max's friend say when he loses a game?
4 What do the ballerinas have to concentrate on?
5 Why does the boy who plays football have to keep fit?

2 Watch the video again. Which two of these things do the children use? What for? What are the other two items used for?

a 
camera

b 
paint brushes

c 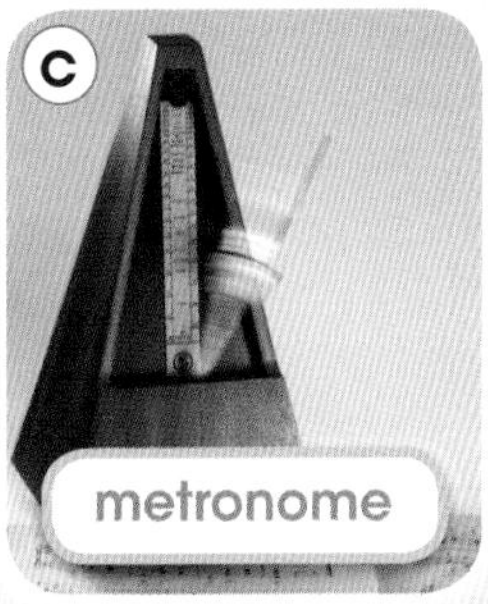
metronome

d 
belt

3 Read, think and answer.

Whole Class

Keep going!

Activities are sometimes difficult, but it's important to keep going. Read these tips. Can you think of any more tips?

- Set a goal.
- Have a positive attitude.
- Don't give up.
- Be patient.
- Keep practising.

4 Work with a partner. Which activities are sometimes difficult for you? Discuss.

a school subject | a sport | a creative activity | another activity

Maths is sometimes difficult for me. What about you?

No, it's not difficult for me.

Key learning outcomes: watch and understand a video about hobbies

21st **Living in the world:** achieving your goals

Unit 3 Healthy habits

Objectives In this unit, I will ...

- name different kinds of food.
- talk about quantity using *too* and *enough*.
- learn about Mexico and the history of chocolate.
- talk about how necessary things are.
- read and write an argument text.
- have a conversation about health and fitness.
- learn how to record information and set a routine.

Hey! A school in Mexico has left a message on the project's website. I wonder how the children make a difference there.

Make a difference

Hi there! My name's Gabriela. I live in Mexico City. It's a huge city and there aren't many places where people can grow their own fruit and vegetables. **My school is helping make a community garden near the school where people can grow food.** We'll know that our fruit and vegetables are fresh and we'll save money, too! We've all helped plant carrots, tomatoes, peppers, pumpkins and potatoes. We've got some fruit trees, too. And sometimes we cook food together. Do you know about Mexican food? Here are some of our favourite ingredients and kinds of food!

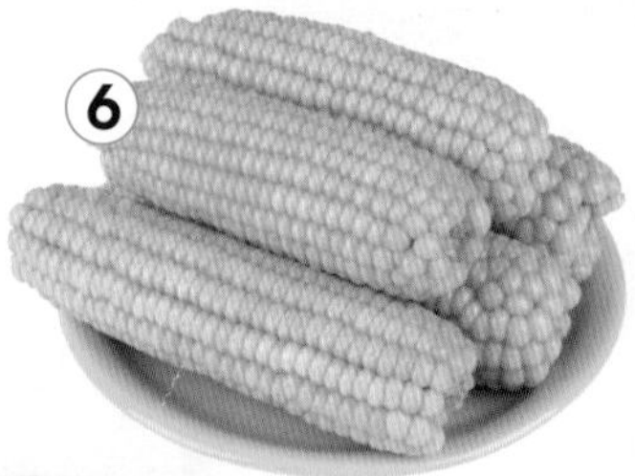

1 Look at Gabriela's photos. Answer the questions. Whole Class

1 What can you see in the photos?
2 Have you ever tasted any of this food?
3 What other food do you like? What's your favourite food?

2 Look and match with photos 1-12. Listen, check and repeat. CD1 33

an avocado beans beef a chilli pepper cinnamon corn garlic prawns a lime an onion peanuts turkey

3 Listen and do the vocabulary quiz. CD1 34

4 Thinking skills Copy the chart. Complete it with food you know.

Food	Shape	Texture	Taste
crisps	round	crunchy	savoury or spicy

Key learning outcomes: identify and say the names of different kinds of food; talk about different food in recipes
Vocabulary: different kinds of food

8

9

10

11

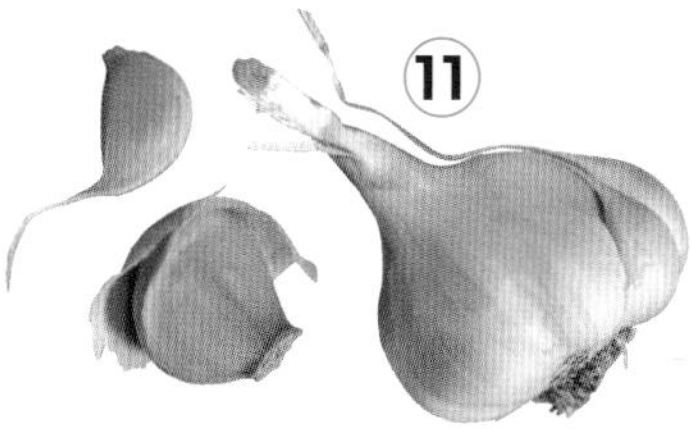

12

5 **Read the rest of Gabriela's message. Which dish do you think you could make?**

We've got some wonderful dishes in Mexico. They taste good and they're bright and colourful, too!

CLASSIC MEXICAN FOOD

This is guacamole. It's a savoury food that you can eat with tortilla chips. It's made with avocados, onions, tomatoes, lime juice, salt and a green herb called coriander. You can add some chilli peppers, too, if you like it spicy!

These are beef tacos. They're easier to make than they look. You cook beef, onions, tomatoes and beans together with some spices. Then put the ingredients in these tacos with any vegetables you like – lettuce or corn, for example.

And how about this for the perfect sweet refreshment on a hot day? Home-made lemonade. Just blend together lemon juice, some lemon peel, sugar and water, then add lots of ice!

6 **Communicate** **Ask and answer about food.**

Are there any tomatoes in guacamole?

Yes, there are.

Is there any sugar in lemonade?

Yes, there is.

1 Describe the photo. What do you think Gabriela is talking about? Read and listen to find out.

CD1 35

Hi, Gabriela. Your community garden sounds fantastic.

Thanks, Tom. Here's a photo of the tomatoes we collected this morning. I think we might have too many tomatoes this year! Many families are going to make tomato sauce to keep in jars.

Wow! That's a lot of tomatoes!

We want to plant some more vegetables, but there aren't enough volunteers here for us to do everything.

Do you grow food all year round?

Yes, but from June to September there's too much rain, so we cover parts of the garden. From November to February there isn't enough rain, so we have to water the plants a lot.

Well, I'm sure it's worth it.

It is! Did you know that another famous food comes from Mexico? I'll send you some information about it.

I wonder what it is. Thanks!

2 Communicate Read and say *true* or *false*. Correct the false sentences.

1 Gabriela says they've got more tomatoes than they need.
2 Gabriela says they've got more volunteers than they need.
3 Gabriela would like less rain from June to September.
4 Gabriela would like less rain from November to February.

3 Look and learn.

Grammar Wall

too & *enough* with countable and uncountable nouns

Countable nouns

There **are too many** tomatoes this year.
There **aren't enough** tomatoes this year.

Uncountable nouns

There **is too much** rain at this time of year.
There **isn't enough** rain at this time of year.

4 Read and think. Choose.

Think about grammar

1 For countable nouns, we use *there is* / *there are* with *too many* / *too much*.
2 For uncountable nouns, we use *there is* / *there are* with *too many* / *too much*.

5 Look at the dialogue in Activity 1 again. Find more examples of *too* and *enough*.

6 Communicate Make sentences about the food in the shop.

There are too many onions in the shop.

There isn't enough rice in the shop.

Key learning outcomes: use *too* and *enough* with countable and uncountable nouns
Grammar: *too* and *enough* with countable and uncountable nouns

Before you read

Gabriela has sent me a story about chocolate. Delicious!

1 Thinking skills — Whole Class

Read and discuss.

- What can you see in the photo on the right?
- Do you like chocolate?
- Do you think chocolate is good for you?
- Do you know how chocolate is made?

2 **Listen and read.** CD1 37

The food of the gods

The story of chocolate started over 2,000 years ago, in a part of Central America which later became Mexico, when farmers discovered the fruit, or pods, of the cocoa tree.

1 They noticed a delicious smell coming from the pods. They took the beans from the pods and dried them. Then they roasted and ground them.

2 They mixed the powder with water and spices to make a cold drink. The chocolate was so good that people believed it was a miracle food.

3 More than a thousand years later, the Spanish explorer, Hernán Cortés, tried the drink. It was very bitter, but he liked it.

4 He brought some beans back to Spain. The King liked the drink, too. Cortés suggested adding sugar, vanilla and cinnamon.

5 The sweet hot chocolate became a big success. People enjoyed sharing it in groups and drinking it on special occasions. However, it was too expensive for poorer people.

6

Chocolate facts

It took until 1847 before people began making chocolate bars. Soon, eating chocolate became much more popular than drinking chocolate!

The cocoa tree can only be grown in warm climates near the equator. A large percentage of the world's cocoa beans grow in Ivory Coast in Africa.

After you read

Go to page 28 in your Activity Book.

Values

- People enjoyed being together as they drank chocolate. When do you eat and drink with groups of friends and family?
- Why is eating together an important way of enjoying time with others?

Key learning outcomes: read a story with a cultural focus; listen for specific information
Values: why eating together is an important way of enjoying time with others

1 Listen and read. Act out. CD1 39

Tom: You need to read this, Jess. It's about the discovery of chocolate in Mexico. They drank chocolate without sugar.

Jess: I can't imagine having chocolate without sugar. It would taste so bitter.

Tom: It was probably healthier to drink chocolate without sugar. Eating too much sugar is bad for you.

Jess: That's true, but you needn't stop eating sugar completely.

Tom: Well, you shouldn't eat too many chocolate bars. Callum needn't worry, he doesn't like chocolate.

Jess: Really? That reminds me, we need to make a cake for Callum's birthday.

Tom: What kind of cake shall we make?

Jess: Well, we mustn't make a chocolate one!

2 Look and learn.

Grammar Wall

Modal verbs

We **need to** make a cake.
You **needn't** stop eating sugar completely.

You **should** go swimming this weekend.
You **shouldn't** eat too many chocolate bars.

We **must** go shopping before the shops close.
We **mustn't** be late.

We can also use **don't need to** instead of **needn't**.

3 Read and think. Choose.

Think about grammar

1 We use **need** *with* / *without* **to** before the verb.
2 We use **needn't** *with* / *without* **to** before the verb.

4 Look at the story on page 31 and the dialogue in Activity 1 again. Find more examples of *need to, needn't* and *mustn't*. What's the difference between *needn't* and *mustn't*?

5 Listen and read. Listen carefully to the contracted forms. Are any of the underlined letters silent? Listen again and repeat. CD1 40

Pronunciation

1 You shou<u>ldn't</u> go to bed without brushing your teeth.
2 You nee<u>dn't</u> put lemonade in the fridge.
3 You mus<u>tn't</u> heat chocolate in a pan.

6 Communicate Use *needn't, mustn't* and *shouldn't* to make sentences about your school. Compare with a partner.

wear a school uniform	arrive late for class
bring a water bottle	run in the corridor
copy your friend's work	use a mobile phone
sit at the front of the class	talk in class

Key learning outcomes: identify and practise saying contracted forms *shouldn't, needn't, mustn't*
Grammar: modal verbs

1 Look and match. Listen, check and repeat. CD1 42

drink fizzy drinks   do exercise   drink water   eat fruit and vegetables
eat junk food   spend time on the computer   rest   go for walks

1 
2 
3 
4 
5 
6 
7 
8 

2 Listen and say *A, B, C* or *D*. CD2 1

Listening tip!
Before you listen, look at the pictures. How are they similar?

1 What does Jane not do every day?

A 
B 
C 
D 

2 What advice does Alfie give to Jane?

A 
B 
C 
D 

3 Listen again. What five questions does Alfie ask? CD2 1

4 Communicate Write the questions. Then ask and answer. Give advice to your partner and give them a healthy lifestyle mark.

Teacher's Resource Bank: Unit 3

Before you read

1 Read and discuss.

Whole Class

- Where do you see people discussing a particular issue?
- Have you watched or read about people arguing their different points of view? What was the argument about?
- Think of some things that people at your school have different opinions about.

2 Look at the photos. What do you think the argument is about? Read and find out.

FAST FOOD No way or OK?

Fast food is made and served very quickly, like burgers and chips, and can be eaten on the street or at home. Is fast food a good thing? We ask two people to give their opinions. What do you think?

LUKE SAYS:

It's no surprise to hear that most fast food is bad for you. It isn't made with fresh ingredients so it hasn't got enough vitamins for a healthy meal. Fast food usually contains a lot of saturated fat, salt and sugar. While many people know this, they carry on buying fast food. Some people say that the high level of salt and other chemicals make the food addictive.

There have also been reports of wood pulp being used to thicken sauces and milkshakes, as well as many unhealthy ingredients. The truth is that we don't always know what we're eating when we buy fast food.

The effect on our health isn't the only issue. We often eat fast food in place of traditional home-made food.

We may start forgetting recipes that are passed on from generation to generation and which make mealtimes special occasions. Fast food is always the same: burgers, chicken nuggets, pizza and chips. It's taking the variety out of our diet.

OLIVIA SAYS:

We've all got busy lives! While I understand that there are healthier food options, fast food helps us carry on with our lives when we're in a hurry. Furthermore, it's cheap. It's usually cheaper than buying the ingredients and cooking a meal.

Some people argue that fast food is unhealthy. In fact, these days there are many rules and regulations for preparing fast food. People who sell fast food have to give a lot of information about the ingredients they use. Fast food restaurants also sell healthier options, such as salads and healthy fruit juices.

Fast food saves time and can taste great!

Reading tip!

Identifying arguments will help you understand the text better.

After you read

3 What do you think?

Whole Class

- Which argument is better? Why?
- Which side of the argument do you agree with?
- What arguments could you add to each side?
- Why is it good to give different opinions on a topic?

Go to page 31 in your Activity Book.

Key learning outcomes: read an argument text; scan the text for specific information; talk about which argument is better

Text type: an argument text

Investigate a text

1 Read and answer.

1 Look at the first sentence of the text in Activity 2. What do you think of this idea?
2 Can you think of arguments that support the idea as well as arguments that are against the idea?
3 Which side of the argument do you think most people in your class would support?

2 Read the text and follow the two sides of the argument.

introduction – what's the topic?

A teacher at our school has suggested beginning every day with 15 minutes of exercise in the school gym.

arguments for this

Firstly, this will make sure everyone does enough exercise every day. Secondly, it will help everyone wake up in the morning. Also, exercise can be a lot of fun.

arguments against this

However, many people walk a long way to school so they've had a lot of exercise already. Furthermore, everyone will need to get changed into their sports kit and back into their school uniform. Some people say that we could use this time more effectively doing something else, like studying for a test.

So, on the one hand, it's good to do more exercise. On the other hand, it will take a lot of time and some children are doing enough exercise anyway. What do you think?

Written by Clare Jones (aged 12)

conclusion – this may include your own opinion

Discuss a text

3 Read the argument text again. Answer the questions. Whole Class

1 How does the writer start the argument text?
2 Does the writer give both sides of the argument?
3 Which time expressions does the writer use to order the events?
4 What phrase does the writer use to give other people's opinions?
5 What phrases does the writer use in the last paragraph to give both sides of the argument?

Writing skills: Using connective words and phrases

When we write a balanced argument, we can use words and phrases to connect sentences.

- To introduce one side of the argument: firstly, secondly, furthermore, also
- To introduce the other side of the argument: however
- To contrast two sides of the argument: on the one hand, on the other hand

4 Look at the two texts again. Find examples of connective words and phrases.

Plan and write your own argument text on page 32 in your Activity Book.

1 **Describe the photos. What is the connection between them?** Whole Class

1

2

3

2 **Listen to the conversation. How does Charlotte keep healthy?** CD2 3

3 **Listen again. Complete the four questions that Finn asks.** CD2 3

- Do you think … ?
- What do you do … ?
- Do you get … ?
- Do you usually … ?

4 **Prepare a conversation about your health on page 33 in your Activity Book.**

Conversation time

When you agree with someone or you do the same things as someone, you can use these phrases.

Yes, I do too.
No, I don't either.
That's the same as me.

Go to the Song Bank, page 125.

5 **Reflect on the unit** **Read and think about your learning. What can you do now?** Whole Class

Hi, Gabriela. Thanks a lot for all the information about Mexico. We've learnt so much.

You're welcome, Tom. I'm glad you enjoyed it. Good luck with the project!

- I can talk about quantities of food.
- I can find Mexico on a map and talk about the history of chocolate.
- I can read and write an argument text.
- I can have a conversation about health and fitness.

Do the Unit Review on page 34 in your Activity Book.

Key learning outcomes: listen to and have a conversation about health and fitness; review learning and reflect on progress in the unit

21 CHANNEL reports

Hi. Today's programme is about running to keep fit. Do you go running? What other things do you do to keep fit?

1 **Watch the video. Read and say *true* or *false*. Correct the false sentences.**

1 Max's dad likes running.
2 A marathon is 25 kilometres.
3 People do cross-country running outside.
4 In the park there is a race every Sunday morning.
5 Katy is a good runner.

2 **Watch the video again. What does Amy say about these different activities?**

3 **Read, think and answer.** Whole Class

Recording information and having a routine

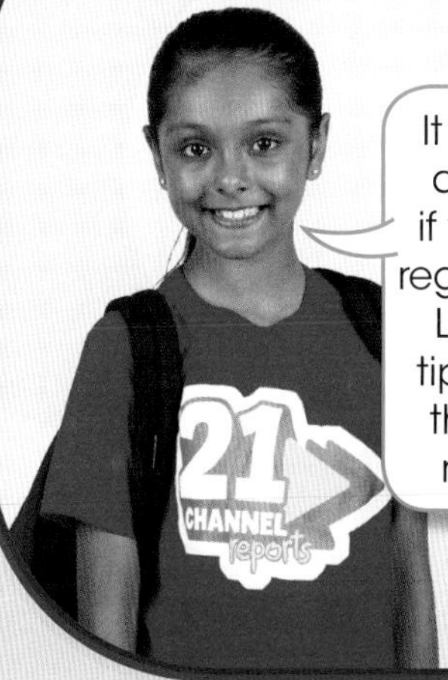

It is easier to do exercise if you have a regular routine. Look at the tips. Can you think of any more tips?

Keep an exercise diary.

Use a calendar to plan your exercise.

Do exercise with a friend. It can be more fun.

Give yourself points for each week you complete the routine!

4 **Work with a partner. Ask and answer about your exercise.**

running | walking | playing tennis / football / basketball | cross-country running

Do you do a lot of exercise?

Yes, I like running. I do athletics every week.

Key learning outcomes: watch and understand a video about keeping fit
21st **Ways of working:** recording information and setting routines

An energy proposal

Prepare a digital presentation about using renewable energy and present it to the class.

Share knowledge

1 Read and discuss. Whole Class

- Do you know where most of our electricity comes from?
- Match the energies with the photos.

coal hydroelectric wind gas solar

- Which of these are sources of renewable energies?

Investigate

2 Listen and complete the notes about renewable energy on page 36 in your Activity Book. CD2 5

3 What are the advantages and disadvantages of each source of renewable energy? Work in pairs or groups. Make notes on page 36 in your Activity Book.

Cooperative learning **Make sure you listen to all members of the group before you write down the ideas.**

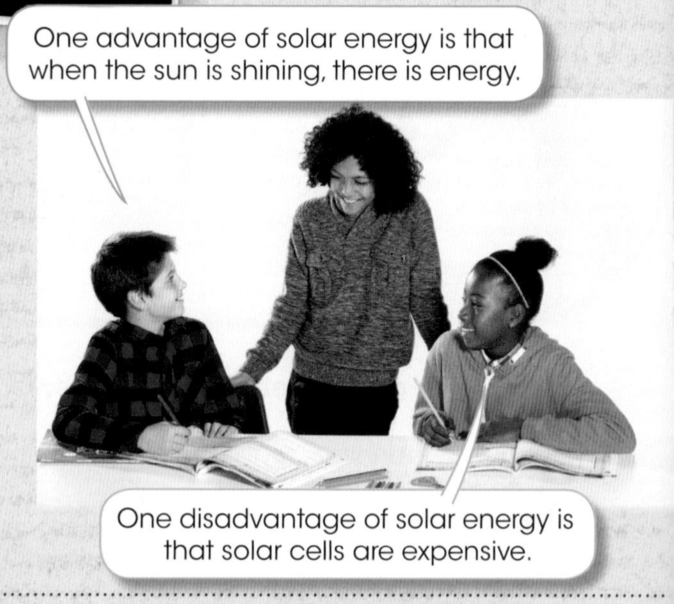

Key learning outcomes: share information about renewable energy; listen and find out about the advantages and disadvantages of renewable energy **Language:** *renewable energy / energies, one advantage is that …*

Plan and create your project

1 **In pairs or groups, propose a renewable energy for your community. Discuss the questions and write your answers on page 37 in your Activity Book.** Whole Class

1 Which renewable energy are you proposing for your community?
2 Why have you chosen it?
3 What could you build?
4 Where could you put it?
5 Is it good for the environment?
6 What could you use the energy for?

Language bank

Let's propose (solar energy) for the community.
We've got (lots of sun here all year).
We could put (wind turbines by the coast).
We could build (two hydroelectric plants).
We could use the energy (to heat the school).

2 **Write and create a digital presentation of your proposal.**

Steps:

1. What key information will you include in the digital presentation?
2. How will you show where the energy is produced and how it connects with the community?
3. What information will you show with photos and pictures, and what will you write?
4. Who's going to do each task?
   - design the presentation
   - write the proposal information
   - research any photos that could be useful
5. What materials do you need?

Present your project

3 **Present your proposal to the class. Take turns to answer any questions.**

Digital tip!
Use the Internet to find out what renewable energy production already exists for your community. ICT

WELL DONE! GIVE ME FIVE!

Reflect on your project

Read and answer the questions on page 37 in your Activity Book.

Key learning outcomes: plan a proposal for your community; write and present the proposal as a digital presentation **Language:** making proposals: *We could (build) ...*

Unit 4 Creative kids

Objectives In this unit, I will ...

- review and learn the names of creative activities.
- make sentences about my favourite books and films using the past passive.
- learn about Japan and Japanese arts.
- ask and answer questions using the past passive.
- read and write a comic strip.
- have a conversation about creative activities.
- learn how to use digital media creatively.

Great! A message has arrived from Japan. I wonder how children make a difference there.

Make a difference

Hi, everyone! My name's Kenji and I live in Ogano. It's a small town in Japan which is famous for its beautiful theatres. Unfortunately, **some children can't go to the theatre because they're in hospital, so my class has decided to perform a puppet show for them next month.** We've already made the puppets and we rehearse the show after school twice a week. It's hard work, but it's good fun. Here's a photo of my puppet. It looks great, doesn't it? I'm also sending you photos of other creative activities that we like to do. I hope you like them.

1 **Look at Kenji's photos. Answer the questions.** Whole Class

1 Do you think these activities are good fun?
2 Which one would you like to do? Why?
3 Which one wouldn't you like to do? Why not?

2 **Look and match with photos 1–12. Listen, check and repeat.** CD2 6

beads puppet do origami clay do traditional dancing perform a play create an animation costume stage make jewellery do ceramics make a film

3 **Listen and do the vocabulary quiz.** CD2 7

4 **Thinking skills** **Read, think and write. Think of more categories.**

List three creative activities that:

... you do with a computer.	... are messy.
... need a lot of energy.	... often have costumes.
... you do with your hands.	... need patience.

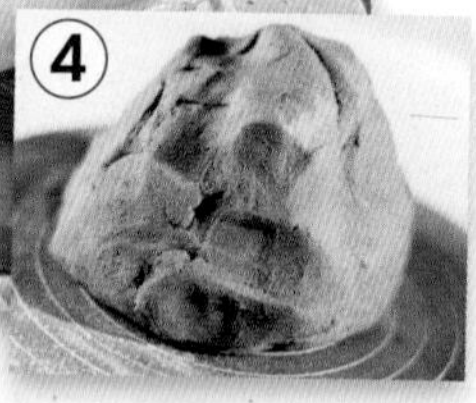

Key learning outcomes: identify and say words associated with creative activities; talk about creative activities **Vocabulary:** creative activities

5 **Read the rest of Kenji's message. Which place would you like to visit? What can you do there?**

Ogano is about 100km from Tokyo. There are lots of things to see and do in the capital city. Here are some of our favourite places.

Museum of Contemporary Art

This amazing art gallery has got special tours for school children so you can learn all about modern art. If you're feeling creative, you can also have a go at producing your own piece of art in one of the cool workshops.

Ghibli Museum

If you're a fan of Japanese animation, then this museum is for you. You can find out how animated films are made and there are lots of hands-on exhibits for children. Don't miss the enormous robot on the museum's roof.

Edo-Tokyo Museum

This museum takes you back in history. You can visit life-size Japanese houses from the past, and you can touch and even ride some of the exhibits. There are traditional dancing shows and you can have a go at a traditional musical instrument, too. It's amazing!

6 **Communicate** **Ask and answer about creative activities.**

Have you ever made a film?

Yes, I have.

When did you do that?

I made a film with my mum's video camera last summer.

1 Describe the photo. What type of puppets are they? Read and listen to find out.

CD2 8

Hi, Kenji. Thanks for the photos. Your puppet looks great, but why is it painted black?

Because it's a shadow puppet. We're going to perform a shadow puppet show at the hospital.

That sounds cool. What do you have to do?

We have to shine a light behind a screen and then use sticks to move the puppets. Look! Here's a photo of how it works.

Wow! It looks amazing. Do shadow puppets come from Japan?

No, they don't. The first shadow puppets were made in China, but they quickly appeared in Japan, too.

And are shadow puppets very old?

Absolutely. The first shadow puppets were created over 1,000 years ago.

That's incredible. Do you like them?

Yes, of course. But I prefer more modern Japanese art. I'll send you some information about that.

2 Communicate Read and say *true* or *false*. Correct the false sentences.

1 The puppets are colourful.
2 The children use strings to move the puppets.
3 Shadow puppets originally came from China.
4 People have used shadow puppets for more than 100 years.

3 Look and learn.

Grammar Wall

Past passive

The puppet **was/wasn't** made last week.

The puppets **were/weren't** painted **by** the children.

Active: The children made the puppets.

Passive: The puppets **were** made **by** the children.

4 Read and think. Choose.

Think about grammar

We use the passive form when we *know / don't know* the name of the person who did the action, or when it *is / isn't* very important.

5 Look at the dialogue in Activity 1 again. Find more examples of the past passive.

6 Communicate Make true sentences.

The *Diary of a Wimpy Kid* books	paint	Beethoven
Jack Sparrow	write	Jeff Kinney
The Mona Lisa	record	Johnny Depp
The 5th Symphony	play	The Beatles
Mickey and Minnie	create	Leonardo da Vinci
Yesterday	compose	Walt Disney

The *Diary of a Wimpy Kid* books were written by Jeff Kinney.

The Mona Lisa wasn't painted by Beethoven.

Key learning outcomes: use the past passive to talk about different forms of art
Grammar: past passive

Before you read

Kenji sent me this information about a Japanese art form called manga.

1 **Thinking skills** Whole Class

Read and discuss.

- Have you ever read any manga comic books?
- What do you know about them?
- Do you think they're entertaining? Why? / Why not?

2 **Listen and read.** CD2 10

Manga

MANGA MAGIC

What is manga?

Manga is a style of art that was originally created by Katsushika Hokusai in Japan more than 200 years ago. Nowadays, manga drawings are like comics that tell stories with pictures and words. When you read manga, you start at the back of the comic and finish at the front. You also read the story frames from right to left.

> **Manga**
> NOUN /ˈmæŋɡə/
> *Man* means amusing and *ga* means picture. When we put these words together it means amusing picture.

What is manga style?

Manga style is easy to recognise because the characters aren't very realistic. They've usually got large eyes, small mouths and tiny noses. Manga characters exaggerate their emotions. When they cry, tears run out of their eyes like water from a tap. When they're angry, they go very red and steam appears around their bodies. Patterns, lines and shapes in the background also help express a character's mood.

What is anime?

When a manga comic book series is very popular, it can be made into an animated series. This is called anime. There are anime films, too. The most famous anime film is called *Spirited Away* and it was made by Studio Ghibli. It won an Oscar in 2003 for the best animated feature film and millions of people around the world have seen it. Another famous anime film is *Your Name*. In 2016, it won best anime film at the Los Angeles Film Critics Awards.

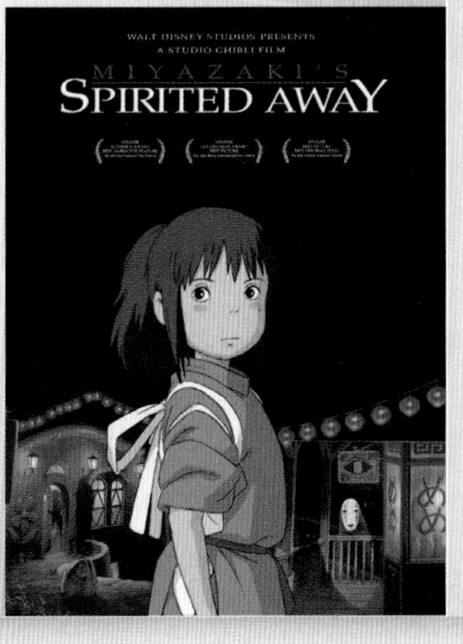

After you read

➔ **Go to page 40 in your Activity Book.**

Values

- **Do you like manga and anime?**
- **Do you like the same comic books and series as your friends?**
- **Is it a problem if your friends like different things?**
- **Why is it important to respect other people's tastes?**

Key learning outcomes: read a story with a cultural focus; listen for specific information
Values: the importance of respecting other people's tastes

1 Listen and read. Act out. CD2 12

Tom: Have you ever read a manga comic book, Jess?

Jess: Yes, I've read lots of them. I collect some manga comics called *Dragon Ball*. Wait a minute, I've got one in my bag.

Tom: It looks really exciting. Who was it written by?

Jess: It was written by Akira Toriyama.

Tom: And when was it published?

Jess: It was first published in 1984.

Tom: That's really old!

Jess: I know, but it's still cool.

2 Look and learn.

Grammar Wall

Past passive questions

When **was** the picture painted?
Who **were** the songs sung **by**?

There are regular and irregular past participles. The regular ones end in *-ed*, but the irregular ones have got different forms.

3 Read and think. Choose.

Think about grammar

To form the past passive, we use the past simple of the verb *be* / *have* + past participle.

4 Look at the dialogue in Activity 1 again. Find examples of questions in the past passive.

5 Listen and read. When is the letter 'w' silent? Listen again and repeat. CD2 13

Pronunciation

1 When was *Diary of a Wimpy Kid* written?
2 Who was *The Sword in the Stone* written by?
3 Where were the two films made?

6 Communicate Ask and answer.

favourite book	Who / write by?
favourite film	When / make?
favourite old song	Who / sing by?
favourite computer game	Where / make?
favourite painting	Who / painted by?

Key learning outcomes: identify and practise words with the silent 'w'
Grammar: past passive questions

1 Look and match. Listen, check and repeat.

CD2 15

actor graffiti artist fashion designer film director
composer photographer sound engineer novelist

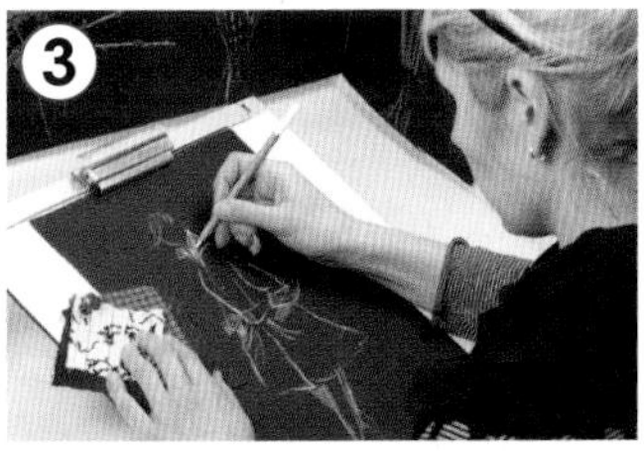

2 Read and choose the correct answers. Listen and check.

CD2 16

Listening tip!

Remember to listen to all the information. The correct answer isn't always the first one you hear.

1 The Eiffel Tower was built by
a Gustave Eiffel b Thomas Eiffel c Leonardo da Vinci

2 *Avatar* was directed by
a Steven Spielberg b George Lucas c James Cameron

3 *Best Song Ever* was sung by
a The Beatles b One Direction c Rihanna

4 *The Hunger Games* was written by
a Stephenie Meyer b Suzanne Collins c J.K. Rowling

5 The role of Belle in the film *Beauty and the Beast* was performed by
a Kristen Stewart b Emma Watson c Jennifer Lawrence

3 Listen again. Which five expressions do the children use to express certainty and uncertainty?

CD2 16

- I'm not very sure.
- I haven't got a clue.
- I've got no idea.
- I definitely know this one.
- I'm not certain.
- I'm sure I know the answer.

4 Communicate Make a quiz. Ask and answer.

Teacher's Resource Bank: Unit 4

Where was *The Hobbit* filmed? Was it filmed in a) France b) New Zealand or c) Scotland?

I'm not very sure. Was it filmed in New Zealand?

Yes, it was. Well done!

Thanks. Now it's my turn to ask you a question.

Key learning outcomes: identify and say expressions for artistic professions; listen for specific information; talk about creative works of art **Vocabulary:** expressions for artistic professions

Before you read

1 Read and discuss. Whole Class

- Where can you read comic strips?
- Why do people enjoy reading them?
- How are they different from other types of writing?
- Which comic strips have you read? What were they about?

2 Look at the title. What do you think happens in the comic strip? Read and find out.

Reading tip!
Think about the different characters in comics. This will help you understand the comic strip.

After you read

3 What do you think? Whole Class

- Do you think this comic strip is funny?
- Which things make it funny?
- Have you got a good imagination like Pat?
- Where do you think missing socks go?

Go to page 43 in your Activity Book.

Key learning outcomes: read a comic for general understanding; scan a review for specific information; discuss comic strips

ext type: **a comic strip**

Investigate a text

1 Read and discuss. Whole Class

Expressions on the characters' faces help us understand what's happening. What do you think these two characters are thinking and saying?

2 Read the comic strip to find out what the characters are thinking and saying.

Discuss a text

3 Read the comic strip again. What do we use to show the following elements? Whole Class

1 a character's words and a character's thoughts
2 what's happening in the story
3 an important noise in the story
4 when a character is angry or surprised

Writing skills: Different punctuation

A full stop (**.**) shows that you've finished a sentence. A question mark (**?**) shows that you've asked a question. An exclamation mark (**!**) shows that you're surprised or angry.

4 Look at the two comic strips again. Find examples of full stops, question marks and exclamation marks.

Plan and write your own comic strip on page 44 in your Activity Book.

Key learning outcomes: identify facial expressions in comics; identify different parts of a comic; write a comic strip; use different punctuation

1 **Describe the photos. Are these activities creative? Why? / Why not?** Whole Class

① 

② 

③ 

④ 

2 **Listen to the conversation. Which creative activity does Sarah do?** CD2 18

3 **Listen again. Complete the four questions that Lucas asks.** CD2 18

• What ...? • What sort ...? • How often ...? • What's the ...?

4 **Prepare a conversation about your creative activities. Use page 45 in your Activity Book.**

Conversation time

Remember to praise people when they tell you about an achievement.

That's amazing!
Well done!
That's fantastic!
I'm impressed.

Go to the Song Bank, page 126.

5 **Reflect on the unit** **Read and think about your learning. What can you do now?** Whole Class

Hi, Kenji. Thanks for sending me so much information about Japan, and good luck with the puppet show.

Thanks, Jess. We're feeling a bit nervous now, but I'm sure it'll be great.

I can talk about books and films using the past passive.

I can find Japan on a map and talk about Japanese arts.

I can read and write a comic strip.

I can have a conversation about creative activities.

Do the Unit Review on page 46 in your Activity Book.

Key learning outcomes: listen to and have a conversation about creative activities; review learning and reflect on progress in the unit

Today's programme is about creativity and technology. What creative things do you do with digital technology?

1 **Watch the video. Read and answer the questions.**

1 What can the fashion designer change?
2 What has the architect drawn?
3 What colour is the graphic designer's car?
4 What animal is in the cartoon?
5 What mustn't you do when you use a computer?

2 **Watch the video again. Which of these digital technologies do you see? Who uses it?**

a

b

c

d

3 **Read, think and answer.** Whole Class

4 **Communicate** **Work with a partner. Which of the creative activities in Activity 3 have you done? Ask and answer.**

Have you ever created a photo story?
Yes, I have.
What was it like?
It was really funny. I did it with my friends at school.

Key learning outcomes: Watch and understand a video about creative technology
21st **Digital skills:** using digital media creatively

Unit 5 Write it down!

Objectives In this unit, I will ...

- name different kinds of messages and communication.
- report what other people have said.
- learn about Egypt and the Rosetta Stone.
- report what others have said about the future and about ability.
- read and write a newspaper article.
- have a conversation about meeting a famous a person.
- learn how to research and present information digitally.

Look! There's a new message from a school in Egypt. Let's read about how their project makes a difference.

Make a difference

Hello, everyone!
My name's Youssef.
Our school is in Alexandria, a city on the north coast of Egypt. Learning to read and write is really important, but many children find it hard to read and write Arabic, our first language. **Some of my friends suggested that the older children could help the younger children.** The teachers thought it was a great idea. Now, 20 of us have got a 'reading friend' who we help twice a week. I think communication with others is really important. Have a look at the pictures of ways that people can send messages and communicate with each other.

1 **Look at Youssef's pictures. Answer the questions.** Whole Class

1 What can you see in the pictures?
2 Have you used any of these ways to communicate?
3 Can you think of any more ways that people send messages or communicate with each other?

2 **Look and match with pictures 1–12. Listen, check and repeat.** CD2 20

advert   blog post   email   greetings card
chat message   cartoon   brochure   leaflet
sign   note   sign language   text message

3 **Listen and do the vocabulary quiz.** CD2 21

4 **Thinking skills** **Copy the chart. Complete it with ways to communicate.**

Communication	Advantages	Disadvantages
Text message	• It's quick. • You can tell people where you are.	• Messages need to be short. • You need to have a mobile phone.

1

2

3

4

5
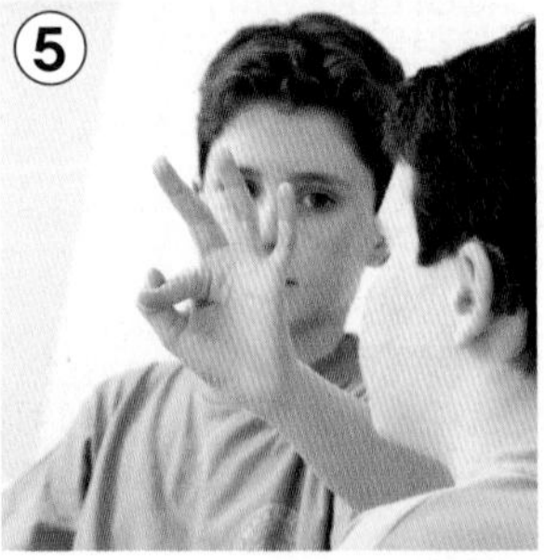

6

7

8

Key learning outcomes: identify and say different kinds of messages and communication; talk about language
Vocabulary: different kinds of messages and communication

Arabic has got a different alphabet to English. Did you know that we read it from right to left? Some English words come from Arabic and other languages. Look at this.

5 **Thinking skills** **Read the rest of Youssef's message. Can you think of any words in your language that come from English?**

The English language has changed a lot in the last thousand years. Most English words come from Greek, French, Latin or German, but some come from other languages, too.

Many food words come from the language spoken in the country where the food comes from. *Burger* comes from German and *pizza* and *pasta* are from Italian. It's more surprising that *orange*, *lemon*, *apricot*, *spinach* and *sugar* all come from Arabic. *Vanilla* comes from Spanish, *coconut* from Portuguese and *ketchup* from Chinese.

QUIZ

Many words for animals are also from different languages.

Can you match the words with the languages?

1 giraffe
2 hamster
3 flamingo
4 guana

a German
b Portuguese
c Spanish
d Arabic

Some ideas were given names by their authors. A Czech man called Karel Capek first used the word *robot* in a play he wrote in 1920. It was very popular and many people started writing about robots – and then people invented them, too.

Much more recently, words like *karaoke* and *manga* have become part of the English language. Which language do they come from?

Answers: *giraffe* from Arabic, *hamster* from German, *flamingo* from Portuguese, *iguana* from Spanish
karaoke and *manga* from Japanese

6 **Communicate** **Ask and answer about language.**

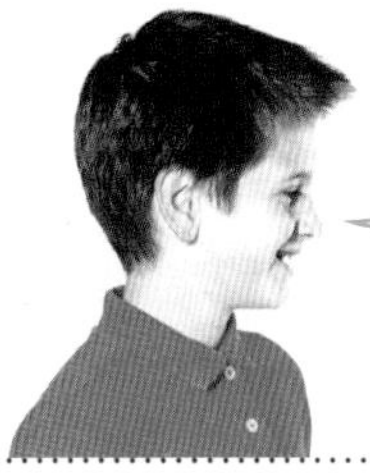

Which language does 'hamster' come from?

It comes from German.

1 **Describe the pictures. What do you think Youssef is explaining? Read and listen to find out.** CD2 22

Hi. That's a great project, Youssef. How's it going?

It's going really well. Our teacher said he was happy with the results. He said the children were better at reading already.

That's brilliant! Is Arabic hard to read?

Yes, there are many different characters to remember. We used these cards to help the children.

What a good idea. Did your teacher help you?

He said the important thing was to help them look carefully at the words and letters.

Are you going to continue helping them?

Yes. Our teacher said we needed to help them with their writing now.

We've suggested the idea at our school, too. The head teacher told us he liked the idea a lot. We might organise it next month.

Good luck! Do you know about the Rosetta Stone? It was discovered near here. I'll send you some information.

Thanks! I look forward to reading about it.

2 **Communicate** **Read the dialogue again. Then read these sentences. Which words change when Youssef tells Callum what his teacher said?**

1 'I'm happy with the results.'
2 'The children are better at reading already.'
3 'The important thing is to help them look carefully at the words and letters.'
4 'You need to help them with their writing now.'

3 **Look and learn.**

Grammar Wall

Reported speech

We use reported speech to say what someone else said.

Direct speech	Reported speech	
'I'm happy with the results.'	He said	he **was** happy with the results.
'I **like** oranges and apples.'	He told me He said	he **liked** oranges and apples.
'They **aren't** very good at tennis.'	She told me She said	they **weren't** very good at tennis.

4 **Read and think. Choose.**

Think about grammar

In reported speech, we change the present to the *past* / *future*.

5 **Look at the dialogue in Activity 1 again. Find more examples of reported speech.**

6 **Communicate** **Ask and answer.**

Billy Helen James Freya

I'm so excited!
I don't want to tidy up.
It isn't raining here.
I like speaking Italian.

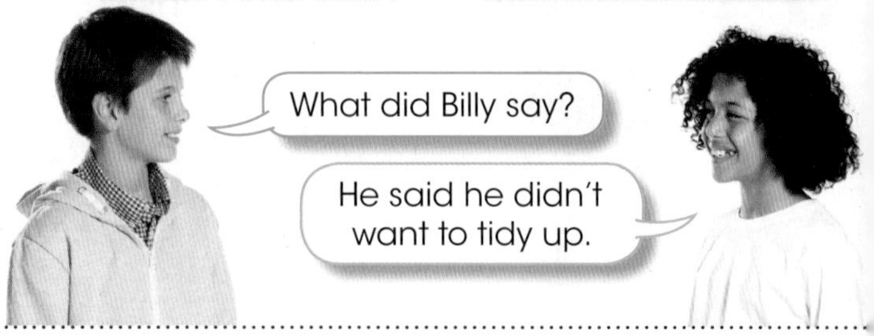

Key learning outcomes: use reported speech to talk about what other people said
Grammar: reported speech

Youssef has sent me some information about the Rosetta Stone.

Before you read

1 **Thinking skills** Whole Class

Read and discuss.

- What can you see in the photo on the right?
- What are hieroglyphics?
- What pictures can you see in the writing?

2 **Listen and read.** CD2 24

CRACKING THE CODE

It looks like a large piece of boring grey rock. So why is the Rosetta Stone so special?

A lucky discovery

For many years, the ancient Egyptians were a mystery because no one could understand the pictures and symbols that they wrote. Then, in 1799, some French soldiers discovered a piece of stone in a village called Rosetta, in northern Egypt. On one side of the stone there was some writing which said the same thing in ancient Greek and in Egyptian hieroglyphics. This meant that the message on the stone was very important for the people in ancient Greece and Egypt. People knew Greek so they could start working out the meaning of the hieroglyphics, but they still couldn't understand all the symbols.

Will anyone find the answer?

The Frenchman, Jean-Francois Champollion, became interested in hieroglyphics at a young age. Someone told him no one could ever understand the symbols. He promised to himself that one day he would solve the mystery.

'I've got it!'

The important moment happened about 23 years after the Rosetta Stone was discovered. Champollion was looking at one word with four symbols. He thought that the first symbol looked like a sun. 'Maybe the first part of the word is the Egyptian word for sun, *ra*,' he thought. Then he realised that the word must be Rameses, the name of an Egyptian pharaoh. He had worked it out! Words sometimes contained other Egyptian words which were shown as a picture. This is similar to writing the word *cartoon* as  **toon.**

Champollion was so excited that he ran into his brother's office and shouted, 'I've got it!' Then he fainted and was ill in bed for five days. Today, you can see the Rosetta Stone in the British Museum in London.

After you read

Go to page 50 in your Activity Book.

Values

- The Rosetta Stone allows us to understand the writings of the ancient Egyptians. What things do you know about the ancient Egyptians, Greeks or Romans?
- Why is it important to learn about these civilisations?

Key learning outcomes: read a story with a cultural focus; listen for specific information
Values: the importance of learning about civilisations

1 **Listen and read. Act out.** CD2 26

Callum: So the Rosetta Stone helped us understand what the ancient Egyptians wrote. That's so cool!

Jess: Yes. We should go and look at it. It's in the British Museum in London. My mum said we could go to London this weekend.

Callum: Great idea!

Jess: My parents said it would rain this weekend, so it's a good idea to go to a museum. What's Tom doing?

Callum: He's drawing some hieroglyphic messages. He said we'd have to try and solve them!

2 **Look and learn.**

Grammar Wall

Reported speech with *will / would & can / could*

'It **will** rain tomorrow.'	He said He told me	it **would** rain tomorrow.
'They **can** read Arabic.'	She said She told me	they **could** read Arabic.

3 **Read and think. Complete.**

Think about grammar

In reported speech, we change the present to the past. We change **will** to ? and we change **can** to ? .

4 **Look at the dialogue in Activity 1 again. Find more examples of reported speech.**

5 **Listen and read. Which word is contracted to 'd. Is it *would* or *could*?** CD2 27

Pronunciation

1 He said he'd arrive home at 12 o'clock.
2 She said she could juggle really well.
3 She told me she wouldn't be at dance club today.
4 He told me he couldn't do his homework.

6 **Report what the children said.**

1 I'll meet Helen after school.
2 I can't answer the question.
3 My dog can swim very well.
4 England won't win the World Cup.

7 **Communicate** **Ask about the things your partner can do. Then tell another partner.**

1 Look and match. Listen, check and repeat. CD2 29

caption front page headline article
sports news interview review
world news fashion section reporter

2 Listen and read. Which parts of the article are true and which are false? CD2 30

Listening tip!
Read the questions carefully before listening.

1. Danny said he hadn't been to England before.
2. He said he liked all English food except for fish and chips.
3. Danny said his character fell in love with Jennifer Lewis's character.
4. He said the film was a comedy.
5. Danny said the final part of the film would make people feel scared.
6. He said he was going to visit Tower Bridge the next morning.

3 Listen again. Complete the questions and sentences that the interviewer uses. CD2 30

- … a few questions?
- … in England?
- … your new film, *Don't Stop!*
- … the final part of the film was really exciting!
- … the rest of your stay?
- … the time to speak to us.

4 Communicate Ask and answer to complete the information about a film star.

Teacher's Resource Bank: Unit 5

Key learning outcomes: identify and say the names of news features; listen for specific information; give information **Vocabulary:** news features

Before you read

1 Read and discuss. Whole Class

- How do you find out about the news in your local area?
- Have you ever read about places or people you know in newspapers or on websites?
- What were the stories about?

2 Read the article quickly. What's it about? Whole Class

Reading tip!
Read the text quickly to get a general idea. Don't worry if you don't understand all the words.

EVERYONE'S CODING!

What do you think the most popular after-school club is in our primary schools? It isn't football or netball, or art or music. It's computer coding.

Learning to program

Chippington Primary School started a coding club last year. It was so popular that they started a second group this year for younger children. John Woodhead, the head teacher, said they'd probably start a third group next year. 'The enthusiasm from the pupils has been incredible.

They don't only want to play on computers, they also want to learn how to program them.'

At coding club, children learn how to program games, animations and robots. The teachers are volunteers who are all professional programmers. The club meets once a week. 'The club is great fun. Last week, the group made a robot lion and learnt how to make it roar,' said volunteer Miranda Davies. 'The pupils are developing skills like problem solving and decision making. And they are working in teams and making friends of different ages so they enjoy it a lot.'

Teachers learn, too!

It isn't just the children who are learning. Many of their teachers said they could now create their own games and animations. 'We've learnt at the same time as the children,' said Leon Spooner, a teacher at the school. 'It's important to keep up with them! It's been fun, too!'

Miranda Davies is one of the volunteers who teach at the coding club.

More volunteers needed

The problem now is that the school needs more volunteers so it can start new groups. Are you a professional programmer who wants to help teach the next generation of coders? Contact Chippington Primary School if you're interested at info@chippington.co.uk

After you read

3 What do you think? Whole Class

- How does this news article make you feel?
- What's the most interesting part of the article?
- How many people's opinions do we hear about?
- Do you think coding clubs are a good idea? Why?

Go to page 53 in your Activity Book.

Key learning outcomes: read a newspaper article for general understanding; scan a newspaper article for specific information; discuss newspaper articles

Investigate a text

1 Read the title of the article in Activity 2. Write six questions you'd like answered by the article using these question words. Whole Class

What ...? | Who ...? | When ...? | Where ...? | Why...? | How ...?

2 Read the article. Does it answer any of your questions?

a fun title

Emma's story is a winner!

one sentence to introduce the news story

Emma Tomkins won first prize in the Radio UK children's story-writing competition, judges announced this week.

reported speech

Emma, 12, in her final year at Martin Primary School, said she was thrilled and surprised. 'I never thought I'd win so this is amazing!' she said.

direct speech

Her story was a mystery about waking up at night. 'Darkness has always interested me so I wanted to write about it,' Emma said.

more details about the news story

She wins £500 worth of books for the school. Head teacher, Linda Knowles, said the whole school was proud of Emma's achievements. 'We love stories at this school so it's fantastic to see one of our pupils winning this prize.'

Emma's story, *The Dark Night*, can be heard on the Radio UK website.

final words, with reference to more information

Discuss a text

3 Read the article again. Answer the questions. Whole Class

1 Is the title of the article good? Why? / Why not?
2 Does the first sentence summarise the story well?
3 Where can you hear Emma's story?
4 How many examples of reported speech are there?
5 How many examples of direct speech are there?
6 What else would you like to find out about the story?

Writing skills: Using *so* to connect sentences

Look at these two sentences: *Darkness has always interested me. I wanted to write about it.*

The second sentence is a result of the first sentence. We can use **so** to connect them: *Darkness has always interested me* **so** *I wanted to write about it.*

4 Look at the two articles again. Find more examples of *so* connecting sentences.

Plan and write your own newspaper article on page 54 in your Activity Book.

Key learning outcomes: identify questions in a newspaper article; identify features of a newspaper article; write a newspaper article; use *so* to connect sentences

1 Describe the photos. What are these people's jobs?

Whole Class

2 Listen to the conversation. Who did Leon meet? What was her job?

CD2 32

3 Listen again. Complete the five questions that Isabel asks.

CD2 32

- Have you … ?
- What … like?
- How … ?
- What … ?
- Would … ?

4 Prepare a conversation about meeting a famous person on page 55 in your Activity Book.

Conversation time

Remember! When you want to think about an answer you can use these phrases before you answer.

I'm not sure. Let me think.
Wait. Let me think.

5 Reflect on the unit Read and think about your learning. What can you do now?

Whole Class

Hi, Youssef. Thanks a lot for all the information about Egypt. We've learnt so much about its history.

No problem. I hope to speak to you again soon!

I can report what someone else has said.

I can find Egypt on a map and talk about the Rosetta Stone.

I can read and write a newspaper article.

I can have a conversation about meeting a famous person.

Do the Unit Review on page 56 in your Activity Book.

Key learning outcomes: listen to and have a conversation about meeting a famous person; review learning and reflect on progress in the unit

21 CHANNEL reports

Hello. Our programme today is about languages. How many languages can you speak? What languages do you learn at school?

1 **Watch the video. Read and say *true* or *false*. Correct the false sentences.**

1 You can hear sign language.
2 Many deaf people use sign language to communicate.
3 The girl shows us the words 'mother' and 'make' in sign language.
4 Sign language is never used in schools.
5 We see children dancing and signing words at the same time.

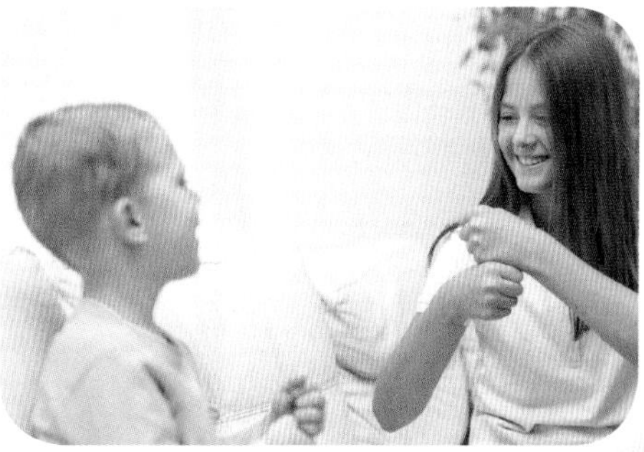

2 **Watch the video again. Match the words to the signs.**

father four eight we

a 

b 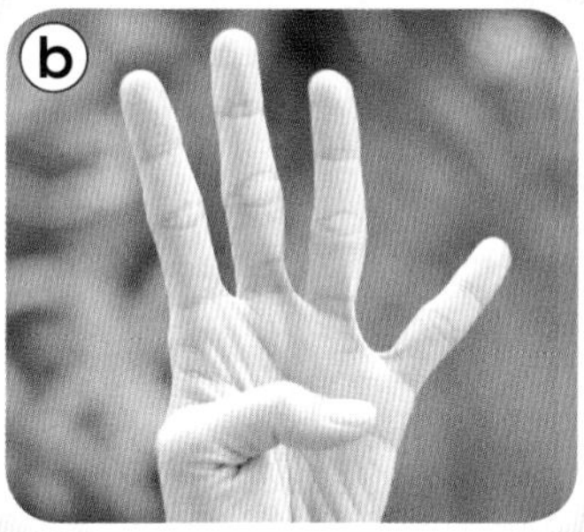

c 

d 

3 **Read, think and answer.** Whole Class

Researching and presenting information digitally

There are many digital tools you can use to research information and then present it to others. What can you use these things for? Can you think of any other tools?

The Internet

A tablet

A mobile phone

A digital whiteboard

4 **Work with a partner. You are going to research and present information about a language. How can you use the tools in Activity 3 to help you?** Brainstorm

We can listen to people speaking the language online.

We can record words using a mobile phone.

Key learning outcomes: watch and understand a video about languages
21st **Digital skills:** using digital media to research and present information

Unit 6 Our future

Objectives **In this unit, I will ...**

- review and learn the names of jobs.
- make predictions about the future.
- learn about Scotland and the story of an amazing musician.
- ask and answer questions that begin with *Do you think ...?*
- read and write a letter for a time capsule.
- have a conversation about what I want to be.
- learn how to think in different ways.

Great! Another message has arrived. It's from a girl in Scotland.

Make a difference

Hi, everyone!
My name's Morag and I live in a small town on the east coast of Scotland. **My classmates love animals so we've decided to help animals.** Every Saturday morning, three pupils go to an animal rescue centre with a teacher and work there. It was my turn last Saturday and I really enjoyed it. My class is also preparing a display about the jobs we want to do when we're older. Here are some of the photos we've collected. I think it would be cool to be a veterinary nurse in the future. What do you think? Do you want to do any of these jobs, too?

1 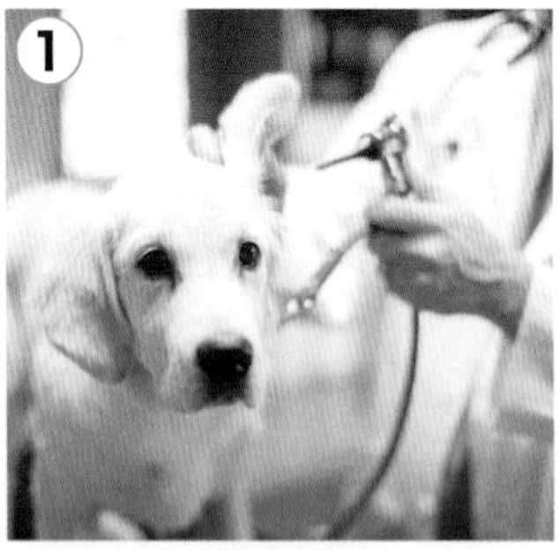

2 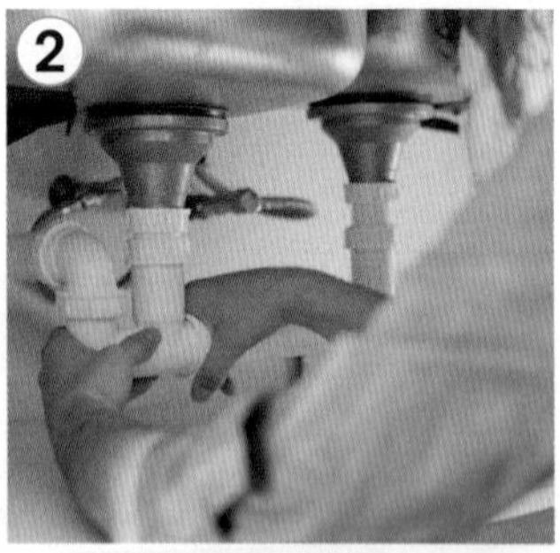

3 

4 

5 

6 

7 

8 

1 Look at Morag's photos. Answer the questions. Whole Class

1 What are the people doing?
2 What are they wearing?
3 Which job looks the most interesting? Why?

2 Look and match with photos 1-12. Listen, check and repeat. CD2 34

archaeologist computer technician politician physiotherapist veterinary nurse plumber detective electrician businessperson security guard tour guide graphic designer

3 Listen and do the vocabulary quiz. CD2 35

4 Thinking skills Read the jobs. Find an odd-one-out in each row.

1 archaeologist, computer technician, physiotherapist

An archaeologist is different because they work outside.

2 politician, plumber, security guard
3 businessperson, veterinary nurse, tour guide
4 detective, electrician, graphic designer

Key learning outcomes: identify and say words associated with jobs; talk about and describe jobs
Vocabulary: names of jobs

9

10
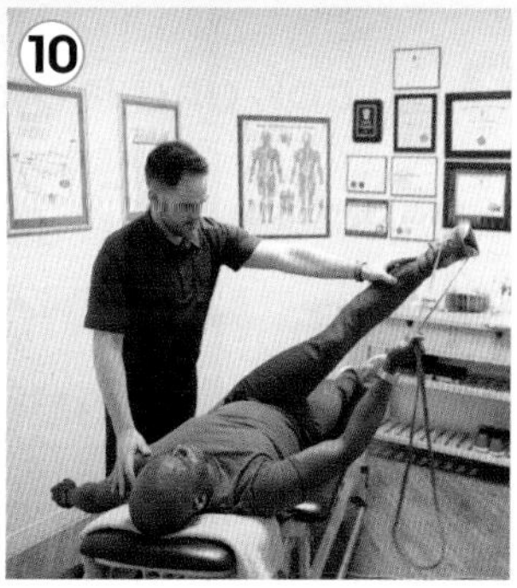
11

12

5 **Read the rest of Morag's message. What job would you like to do? Why?**

Volunteering is good fun and you can learn new skills, too. Look at the information on the animal rescue centre's web page.

Animal Rescue Shelter

home | cats | dogs | volunteers | links

Are you aged 12–16? Have you got some free time and lots of energy?

We need …

… young photographers to take photos of pets when they arrive at the centre. These photos help us find new homes for the animals.

… young journalists to help write our newsletters. These newsletters inform people about the work we do.

… young animal carers to hold and brush the pets. This helps the pets feel calm and loved.

… young graphic designers to help design posters and work on our web page. This includes uploading photos of the new pets and updating the pet adoption list.

You can make a big difference to animals' lives. Find out about volunteering today!

6 **Communicate** **Play a game. Can you guess the job in five questions?**

1 Describe the photo. What do you need to be good at to be an astronaut? Read and listen to find out. CD2 36

Hi, Morag. Your project sounds fantastic.

Thanks, Tom. I love being with the animals.

Is that why you want to be a veterinary nurse when you're older?

Absolutely. What about you? Do you know what you want to be?

Well, my dream is to be an astronaut like the one in this photo.

What a great job. Is it difficult to be an astronaut?

Yes. It's almost impossible so I probably won't be one.

Are you good at Maths and Science?

Yes, I am.

So you might be an astronaut in the future.

Hmm! I suppose so.

I know. I'll send you a story about an amazing woman and her work. That will make you feel more positive.

2 Communicate Read the dialogue again. Ask and answer.

1 What does Tom want to be when he's older?
2 Does he think it's possible?
3 Why does Morag think it's possible?
4 What's Morag going to send Tom?

3 Look and learn.

Grammar Wall

Making predictions about the future

We use **will** and **won't** when we're certain about the future. We can use the adverbs **probably** and **definitely**, too.

I **will definitely** be an archaeologist.
I **probably won't** be a politician.

When we aren't sure about the future, we use **may**, **might** and **could**.

I **may/might/could** be a chemist.

0%				100%
definitely won't	probably won't	may/might/could	will probably	will definitely

4 Read and think. Choose.

Think about grammar

The verbs **will**, **won't**, **may**, **might** and **could** are always followed by an *infinitive verb* / *verb + -ing*.

5 Look at the dialogue in Activity 1 again. Find more examples of future predictions

6 Communicate Talk about the jobs.

veterinary nurse musician electrician teacher detective firefighter artist

Key learning outcomes: making predictions about the future
Grammar: *will, won't, may, might, could* followed by an infinitive

Before you read

Morag sent me this story about a famous musician called Evelyn Glennie.

1 **Thinking skills** Whole Class

Read and discuss.

- Which instruments can you see in the photo?
- Have you ever played a musical instrument?
- What are the qualities of a good musician?

2 **Listen and read.** CD2 38

The story of Evelyn Glennie

Evelyn Glennie was born in Aberdeenshire, Scotland. Her parents played instruments in a traditional Scottish dance band.

1 When she was eight, Evelyn began studying the piano. She was a brilliant music student, but soon after she started having problems with her hearing.

2 By the time Evelyn was 12, she was deaf. This was a difficult time for her. But one day, while she was watching a school concert, she had an idea.

3 Evelyn wanted to learn to play the drums. Her music teacher showed her how to feel a drum's vibrations with her fingertips and through her bare feet.

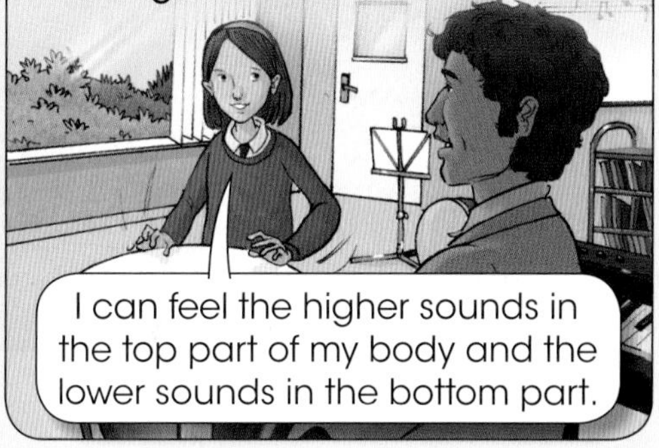

4 Evelyn studied percussion and when she was 19, she won an important award. However, she didn't stop there.

5 She worked hard to achieve her dream. Now she performs about 100 solo concerts around the world every year and she has won more than 80 international awards. She also plays the xylophone, the chimes and many more percussion instruments.

There are no limits for Evelyn. What do you think she'll do next?

After you read

Go to page 60 in your Activity Book.

Values

- Why was it a difficult time for Evelyn when she was 12?
- What did she decide to do?
- Do you think there have been a lot of challenges in her life?
- Is it important to be positive when there's a challenge? Why?

Key learning outcomes: read a story with a cultural focus; listen for specific information
Values: the importance of being positive when there's a challenge

1 Listen and read. Act out.

CD3 2

Callum: That was a brilliant story. I really admire strong people.

Tom: I know. You play a musical instrument, too, don't you?

Callum: Yes, I play the guitar.

Tom: Do you play well?

Callum: I'm not bad. Listen to this.

Tom: Wow! You're really good. Do you think you'll play in the school concert next month?

Callum: Yes, I probably will.

Tom: And do you think you'll be famous in ten years' time?

Callum: If I keep on practising, who knows?

2 Look and learn.

Grammar Wall

Embedded questions

Do you think	I/you he/she we/they	will	be famous? pass the exam? speak English?

Remember that when we start a question with **Do you think ...?**, the rest of the sentence is in the affirmative.

3 Read and think. Choose.

Think about grammar

1 When we say **one hour's time**, the apostrophe goes *before* / *after* the 's'.
2 When we say **two hours' time**, the apostrophe goes *before* / *after* the 's'.

4 Read the story on page 63 and the dialogue in Activity 1 again. Find more examples of embedded questions.

5 Listen and read the sentences. When does the intonation go up and down? Listen again and repeat.

CD3 3

Pronunciation

1 I might go to the beach in August.
2 I definitely won't go to school on Saturday.
3 I could study Chinese in ten years' time.
4 I'll probably go shopping next week.
5 I may play football at break time.

6 Communicate Make questions. Ask and answer.

drive a car	this evening
watch cartoons	the day after tomorrow
make a film	next week
use a computer	in three months' time
learn to fly	in one year's time
travel in space	in ten years' time
have a job	in 20 years' time

Key learning outcomes: identify and practise rising and falling intonation patterns with modal verbs of possibility and certainty
Grammar: using embedded questions

1 Look and match. Listen, check and repeat. CD3 5

go to university | leave home | get a job | go backpacking
get married | start a business | learn to drive | have children

1

2

3

4

5

6

7

8

Listening tip!
Look at the pictures and guess what words could be used to describe them.

2 Listen and say *A, B* or *C*. CD3 6

1 Will Sally go to university in the future?
- A She'll probably go to university.
- B She probably won't go to university.
- C She will go to university.

2 Will Sally learn to drive in the future?
- A She'll definitely learn to drive.
- B She probably won't learn to drive.
- C She'll probably learn to drive.

3 Will Sally go backpacking in the future?
- A She might go backpacking.
- B She probably won't go backpacking.
- C She will definitely go backpacking.

4 Will Sally start a business in the future?
- A She'll definitely start a business.
- B She probably won't start a business.
- C She could start a business.

3 Listen again. Which expressions does Sally use to express doubt? CD3 6

• I don't know. • I'm not sure. • I doubt it. • You never know. • I don't think so.

4 Communicate Predict your partner's answers. Then ask questions to check your predictions.

Teacher's Resource Bank: Unit 6

Do you think you'll go to university in the future?

Yes, I'll probably go to university in the future.

My prediction is right. That's one point for me.

Key learning outcomes: identify and say expressions for talking about life events; listen for specific information; talk about the future **Vocabulary:** expressions for life events

Before you read

1 Read and discuss. Whole Class

- What's a time capsule?
- Where do people usually put a time capsule?
- Which objects are going to go in this time capsule?
- Which objects would you put in a time capsule?

2 Look at the date on the time capsule letter. How long ago was it written? Predict what's in the letter. Read and find out.

Reading tip!
Read the text quickly to get a general idea. Underline unknown words and ask your teacher.

Greenhill Primary School
5th September 1980

To the finder of this time capsule,

Hello from the past! My name is Sandra Jones and I'm 11 years old. This letter was buried in a time capsule by my class in the school playground in 1980.

Life in 1980 is good fun. I go to school from nine o'clock to half past three, and after school I play outside with my friends. I love riding my BMX bike and playing an amazing new puzzle called a Rubik's cube. I also like listening to my music cassettes, playing arcade games and going to the cinema. My favourite possession is my digital watch. It looks really modern and you can use it as a calculator, too! Do they still exist in your time?

I imagine that life will be very different in the future. I think that robots will work in factories and children will use computers in school. I also think that people will have holidays in space. Am I right?

Finally, I've got some wishes for the future. I hope that there aren't any wars and that there are new cures for diseases in your time.

Good luck in the future!

Sandra Jones

After you read

3 What do you think? Whole Class

- How old is Sandra now?
- Is life similar for children now?
- What was different about life then?
- Are Sandra's predictions for the future correct?
- Have her wishes come true?
- Is it a good idea to make a time capsule?

Go to page 63 in your Activity Book.

Key learning outcomes: read an informal letter for general understanding; scan an informal letter for specific information; discuss a letter

Investigate a text

1 **Look at the contents of this time capsule. What do they tell us about the owner?** Whole Class

2 **Read the time capsule letter to find out.**

address and date

6 High Street, Oxford
9th September 2017

greeting

To the finder of this time capsule,

Hello from the past! My name is Tom Stanley and I'm 12 years old. This letter comes from a time capsule buried in my garden in 2017.

Life in 2017 is great. I go to school from nine o'clock to four o'clock, and then I usually do my homework or go to football training. I'm mad about football! In my free time, I love reading comic books and listening to music, too. My favourite possession is my MP3 player. Do they still exist in your time?

I imagine that life will be very different in the future. I think that there will be solar-powered mobile phones and that people will watch zero gravity games in big stadiums. Am I right?

Finally, I've got some wishes for the future. I hope that there are more jobs and that there are houses for everyone.

body

Good luck in the future!

closing message

Tom Stanley

signature

Discuss a text

3 **Read the letter again. Answer the questions.** Whole Class

1 Where do you write the address and the date?
2 How many paragraphs are in the body of the letter?
3 How does the writer finish the letter?
4 Are the contents of the letter interesting?

Writing skills: Paragraphs

A paragraph is a group of sentences in a piece of writing. Each paragraph introduces new information or a new point of view.

Remember that when we begin a paragraph, we need to start writing on a new line.

4 **Read the two letters again. What information appears in each paragraph?**

Plan and write a time capsule letter on page 64 in your Activity Book.

Key learning outcomes: identify the format of an informal letter; write an informal letter using paragraphs

1 Describe the photos. What do these people do in their jobs? Whole Class

1

2

3

4

2 Listen to the conversation. What does Eva want to be when she's older? Why? CD3 8

3 Listen again. Complete the four questions that Joe asks. CD3 8

- What … when you're older?
- What … do?
- Why…?
- Is …?

4 Prepare a conversation about a job you'd like to do on page 65 in your Activity Book.

Conversation time

Remember! Use the expression *What else?* to find out more information.

What else do they do?
What else do you need to do?

Go to the Song Bank, page 126.

5 Reflect on the unit Read and think about your learning. What can you do now? Whole Class

Hi, Morag. Thanks for sending all the information about jobs. I've learnt a lot and I think you'll be a brilliant veterinary nurse one day.

Thanks, Tom. I've had fun thinking about the future, too. Speak again soon!

I can make predictions about the future.

I can find Scotland on a map and talk about an amazing musician.

I can read and write a letter for a time capsule.

I can have a conversation about what I want to be.

Do the Unit Review on page 66 in your Activity Book.

Key learning outcomes: listen to and have a conversation about what I want to be; review learning and reflect on progress in the unit

21 CHANNEL reports

Today's programme is about the future. Do you think technology will be different in the future?

1 **Watch the video. Read and answer the questions.**

1 Why are the seats in the first car special?
2 Why is the second car special?
3 Where does the first drone leave the parcel?
4 What can the first robot in the video do?
5 What will people need to see computer screens in the future?

2 **Watch the video again. How will these activities change in the future?**

a
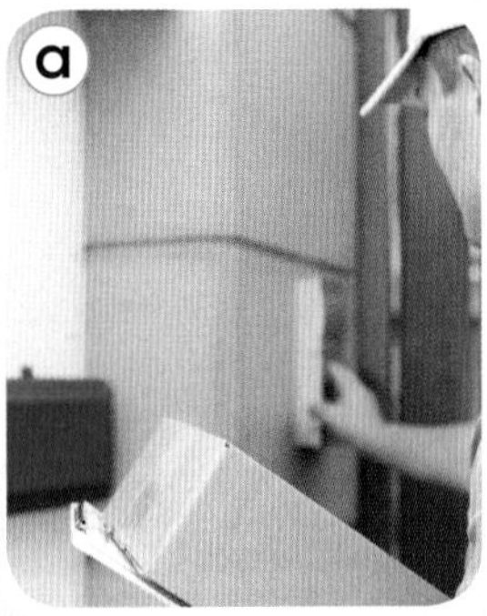

b

c

d

3 **Read, think and answer.** Whole Class

Thinking outside the box

When you think outside the box, you create new and original ideas. Read these tips. Can you think of other tips?

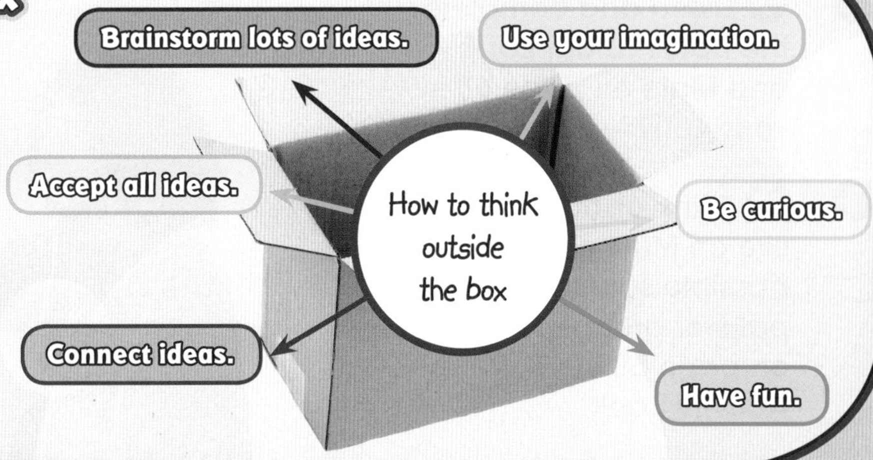

4 **Work with a partner. Read and brainstorm ideas. Think outside the box!** Brainstorm

Think of ...

1 ... five new ingredients for a sandwich.
2 ... five new school subjects.
3 ... five decorations for the classroom.

We can have avocado as a new ingredient for a sandwich.

We can have skateboarding as a new subject.

Key learning outcomes: Watch and understand a video about the future
21st **Ways of thinking:** thinking in different ways

Living on Mars

Design a home to survive on Mars and present it to the class.

Share knowledge

1 Read and discuss. Whole Class

- What are the things that allow us to live on Earth?
- Look at the words. Why are these things important?

temperature   the Sun   water   atmosphere   energy

- Do any of these conditions exist on Mars?

Investigate

2 Listen and complete the notes about Earth and Mars on page 68 in your Activity Book. CD3 10

3 Think about why we can't live on Mars. Find out about possible solutions. Work in pairs or groups. Make notes on page 68 in your Activity Book. Brainstorm

Cooperative learning

Work together to think of original ways of presenting the ideas. It's good to be creative.

Key learning outcomes: share information about living conditions on Earth and Mars; discuss possible solutions to the problems of living on Mars **Language:** conditions for life, needs and possibilities

Plan and create your project

1 ➔ **Your group is going to design a home on Mars. Discuss the questions. Write the information on page 69 in your Activity Book.** Whole Class

1 What would the house look like?
2 What would you have inside the house?
3 Where would you grow food?
4 Where would you get water?
5 What would you wear?
6 How would you travel around?
7 Where would you get energy?

Language bank

Let's grow (fruit) here.
We would wear (spacesuits).
We would travel in (special cars).

2 **Prepare a presentation of your design.**

Steps:

1. What's the key information for your project?
2. What's the best way of presenting this information? Will you draw or write about the design?
3. Who's going to do each task?
4. What materials do you need and where will you get them from?

Present your project

3 **Present your design to the class. Take turns to answer any questions.**

Before your presentation, check some of your ideas on the Internet. Use search questions like: What material can protect you from ultraviolet rays? ICT

➔ **Read and answer the questions on page 69 in your Activity Book.**

WELL DONE! GIVE ME FIVE!

Unit 7

Buying and selling

Objectives **In this unit, I will ...**

- learn words related to money and shopping.
- compare things using *too*, *enough* and *as*.
- learn about the USA and fair trade.
- use *if* and *will* to talk about actions and results in the future.
- read and write an advert.
- have a conversation about money.
- learn about entrepreneurial skills.

Have a look at this! It's a message from a school in the USA. Let's see how their project makes a difference.

Make a difference

Hello, everyone! My name's Kelvin. Our school is in Pittsburgh, a city in Pennsylvania. At school, we had a talk about saving money by recycling our things. We all grow out of our toys and clothes, but they can still be used by other people. **So we've organised an 'almost-new' sale** where families can sell items they don't want anymore. It's great for buyers and sellers. Everyone saves money! It's also good for the environment because fewer things are thrown away. Here are some photos related to money. Which ones do you think we'll see at our 'almost-new' sale?

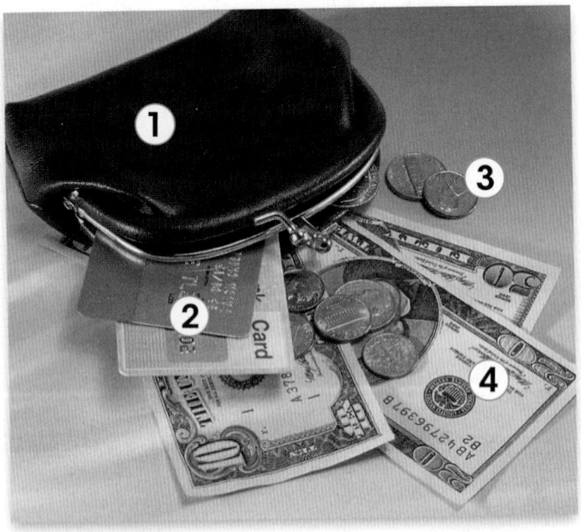

1 **Look at Kelvin's photos. Answer the questions.** Whole Class

1 What can you see in the photos?
2 Where do you and your family go shopping?
3 Do you or your family buy things online? Do you prefer shopping online or in a shop?

2 **Look and match with photos 1–12. Listen, check and repeat.** CD3 11

cashier coins credit card customer
moneybox banknotes price tag purse
till receipt save money spend money

3 **Listen and do the vocabulary quiz.** CD3 12

4 **Thinking skills** **Copy the chart. Complete it with three things you've bought. Compare your answers with a partner.**

Item				Did you use your own money?			
How much did it cost?				Where did you buy it?			

Key learning outcomes: identify and say words associated with money and shopping; talk about an 'almost-new' sale **Vocabulary:** money and shopping

5 **Read the rest of Kelvin's message. Would you like to take part in a sale like this? What would you sell?**

Here's some information about how the sale works. I'm going to help count the money. Do you know what currency we use in the USA? It's 'dollars'. Here are a few facts!

OUR 'ALMOST-NEW' SALE!

HOW DOES IT WORK?

1. Decide what to sell. Make sure that …
   - clothes are clean and folded. We particularly welcome fancy dress!
   - toys and games have got no broken or missing parts.
   - DVDs and books are suitable for 12-year-olds.
2. Complete the registration form.
3. We'll send you a selling number. Put a price tag on every item, and include your selling number and the price you'd like to sell each item for.
4. Put everything in a box and bring it to the sale.
5. We keep all the price tags at the till and, at the end, we work out how much money you've earned. We then give you the money.

THE DOLLAR

The largest banknote used is $100.

American coins have got names. A five-cent coin is called a **nickel**. A ten-cent coin is called a **dime** and a 25-cent coin is called a **quarter**.

6 **Communicate** **Think about the 'almost-new' sale. Ask and answer.**

What would you sell at the sale?

I'd sell my red cap. It's too small for me.

How much would you sell it for?

Hmm! One euro.

1 Describe the photo. Why do you think Kelvin has included it? Read and listen to find out.

CD3 13

Hi, Kelvin. The 'almost-new' sale sounds like a really worthwhile project. Has there been a lot of interest?

Yes, there has! We've had to move the event to a bigger hall. The school hall isn't big enough to fit all the tables.

That's great news. How do people know how much they can sell things for?

We give everyone a guide. Things at the sale aren't as expensive as in the shops of course!

Is your family selling anything?

Yes. We're selling my teddies. Look at them! I'm too old to play with them now!

What kinds of things do you want to buy?

For me, it's more important that the event goes well and fairly. We've been learning about how fair trade started. I'll send you some information.

Thanks! That sounds interesting.

2 Communicate Read and say *true* or *false*. Correct the false sentences.

1 The prices at the sale are higher than in the shops.
2 They aren't going to have the sale in the school hall because it's too small.
3 The teddies are for children younger than Kelvin.
4 Kelvin wants the sale to be as fair as possible.

3 Look and learn.

Grammar Wall

Comparative forms

I'm **too** old to play with teddies now.

He is/isn't old **enough** to buy a mobile phone.

My sister is **(not) as** tall **as** her friends.

4 Read and think. Match.

Think about grammar

Can you match the sentences with the similar meanings?

1 It isn't as small as a mouse.
2 It's as small as a mouse.

a It's the same size as a mouse.
b It's bigger than a mouse.

5 Look at the dialogue in Activity 1 again. Find examples of these comparative forms.

6 Communicate Look at the pictures and make sentences.

expensive big tall old

In this picture, the blue T-shirt isn't as expensive as the red one.

In this picture, the plant …

1

2

3

4

Key learning outcomes: use comparative forms to make comparisons
Grammar: comparative forms

Before you read

Kelvin says that the idea of fair trade began in his home state of Pennsylvania. Let's find out about it.

1 Thinking skills Whole Class

Read and discuss.

- What kinds of things do people grow or produce in poor countries?
- What problems might there be for these people?
- *Trade* is the word for buying and selling things. What do you think 'fair trade' is?

2 **Listen and read.** CD3 15

TRADING FAIRLY WITH OTHERS

Who was the first person to help people in poor countries improve their trade? Some say it was Edna Ruth Byler.

In the 1940s, Edna was living in a small town in Pennsylvania, USA. She worked as a volunteer for a charity. In 1946, she travelled to Puerto Rico, an island in the Caribbean. She was shocked that the people were too poor to live comfortably. They had very little money and she wanted to find a way to help.

Edna had an idea. She loved the materials that the people were sewing and thought that the materials in the USA weren't as beautiful. She decided to buy some and then sell them to people in the USA. The craftspeople were pleased. 'If you sell them all, we'll make more for you,' they said. Edna travelled from town to town and sold things from the boot of her car. She was a good salesperson and returned to Puerto Rico for more materials.

Edna was paying a fair price to the craftspeople and this helped them live better and improve their trade. Over the next 30 years, she worked with craftspeople in many poor countries. She suggested the kinds of crafts that would sell well in the USA and helped organise their trade.

There are many organisations now that help people in poorer countries improve their trade. They work with farmers of coffee, sugar, bananas and many other kinds of food in Asia, South America and Africa. They help them organise their production and teach their skills to each other so that their business can grow. The organisations also make sure that the producers are paid a fair price for the food and that this price doesn't suddenly go down.

After you read

Go to page 72 in your Activity Book.

Values

- Edna Ruth Byler showed a lot of initiative to help the people in Puerto Rico. What's 'initiative' and why is it important?
- Give some examples of when you've shown initiative.

Key learning outcomes: read a story with a cultural focus; listen for specific information
Values: the importance of showing initiative

1 Listen and read. Act out. CD3 17

Tom: Kelvin's information was really interesting. It's great that people try to help poorer countries trade successfully.

Jess: Yes. I've found out a lot more about Fairtrade. If something is from Fairtrade producers, it'll have a FAIRTRADE Mark on it.

Tom: So do your family only buy Fairtrade products?

Jess: Not always. If we buy Fairtrade products, it'll help the workers in poorer countries. But the products are sometimes more expensive.

Tom: Look at these T-shirts. They've got a FAIRTRADE Mark on them.

Jess: The cotton must be from Fairtrade producers.

2 Look and learn.

Grammar Wall

First conditional

If we buy Fairtrade products, it'll help the workers in poor countries.

If I finish my homework early, I'll play games on the computer.

One or both of the verbs can be in the negative:

If it **doesn't** rain, we'll play tennis.

If you **don't** buy a ticket, you **won't** win a prize.

What will you do if you miss the bus this afternoon?

3 Read and think. Complete.

Think about grammar

We use the first conditional to predict what will happen after a hypothetical action in the future.

We use *if* + **?** simple to describe the action, and the **?** + infinitive to describe the result.

4 Read the article on page 75 and the dialogue in Activity 1 again. Find more examples of the first conditional.

5 Listen and read the sentences. Look at the blue letters. Do you repeat these sounds in the second word? Listen again and repeat. CD3 18

Pronunciation

If it doesn't rain, I'll leave the bikes outside.

If you eat too much at night, you won't sleep well.

6 Say the sentences, linking the same sounds. Listen and check. CD3 19

1 If you keep practising, you'll get better.
2 He'll be angry if you don't take out the rubbish.
3 If it's hot tomorrow, we'll take caps and sun cream.

7 Communicate Are you superstitious? In your country, do people say that these things bring good luck, bad luck or nothing at all?

1

If you open an umbrella in the house, you'll have bad luck.

2

3

4

5

1 Look and match. Listen, check and repeat. CD3 21

bent cracked faulty loose ripped scratched stained

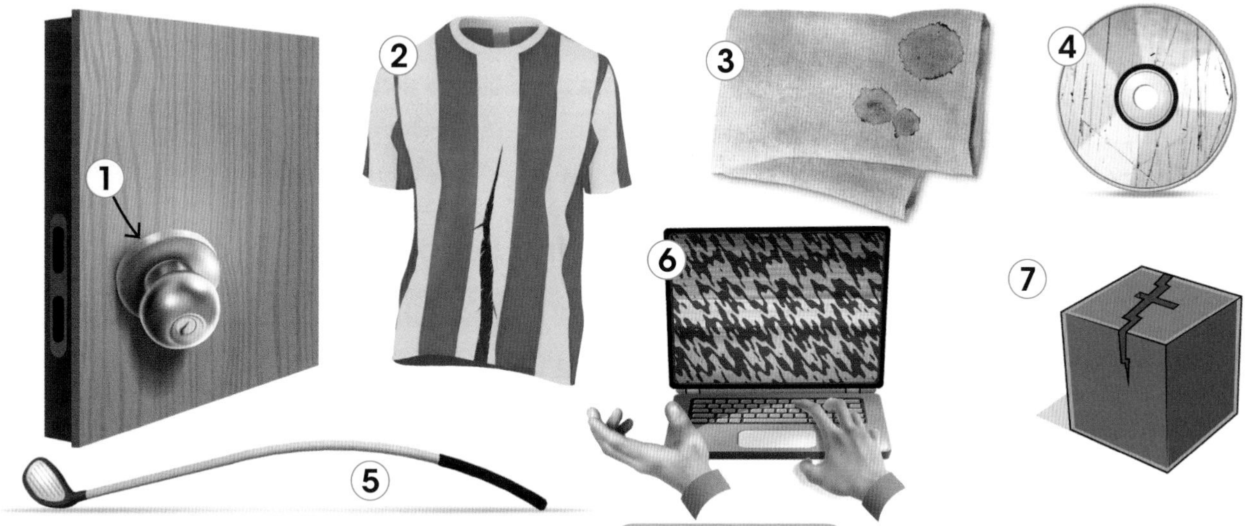

Listening tip!
Before you listen, think of how you describe the items in the pictures in English.

2 Listen and say *A*, *B* or *C*. CD3 22

1 Which kite did Annie buy?

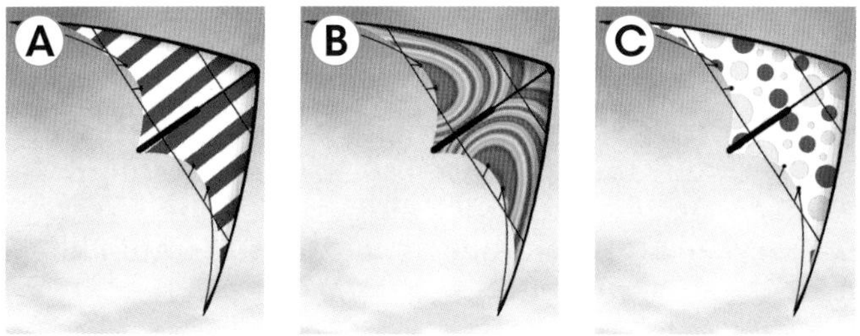

2 Which of these is <u>not</u> a problem with the tent?

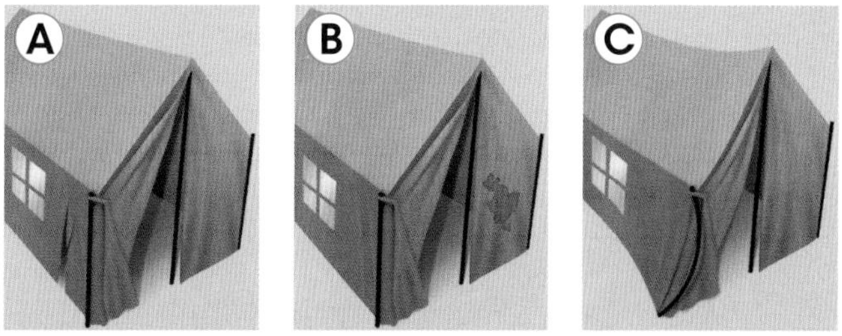

3 Listen to the conversation in the camping shop. What happens in the end? CD3 23

4 Listen again. Who uses these expressions, the customers or the shop assistant? CD3 23

- There are some problems with it.
- I'm sorry to hear that.
- Can I see your receipt?
- Would you like your money back?
- Could we have another one?
- We'll check it.

5 Communicate Ask and answer to complete the chart.

Teacher's Resource Bank: Unit 7

Key learning outcomes: identify and say expressions related to describing damaged objects; listen for specific information; talk about damaged goods **Vocabulary:** phrases related to damaged objects

Before you read

1 Read and discuss. Whole Class

- Where have you seen adverts for these things?

breakfast cereal | cars | toys | films

- What do adverts try to do?
- When have adverts persuaded you to do something?

2 Look at the photos. Which would you most like to try? Read and see if you still feel the same way.

Reading tip!
Try and guess unknown words by reading the context of the sentence.

This week's special offers ...

TIGER WAVEBOARDS

Ride the tiger and don't look back!

Have you ever used a waveboard? If not, you're missing out! Pick up a Tiger Waveboard today. We think they'll be as popular as skateboards. You can turn more easily and more sharply than on a skateboard and, more importantly, you don't need to put your foot on the ground to push yourself along. It takes minutes to learn and you'll have fun for years! These beginner boards are great value and make excellent presents for active teenagers. Buy one now before we run out!

Swoop Stunt Kites

Switch to a swoop!

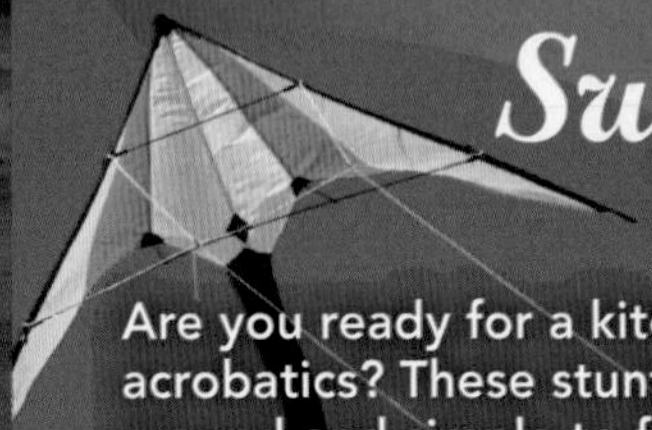

Are you ready for a kite that can perform first-class acrobatics? These stunt kites are the coolest! Light to carry around and simple to fly, they come in a variety of bright colours. The sail is made of strong polyester so it won't rip. The fibreglass rods are flexible so they'll bend, but they won't break. When you buy a kite, you'll receive a free DVD of special tricks so you can impress your friends with your dives and loops. Rush out and buy one now! If you buy two, you'll get a 10% discount!

THE SPLASH 500

The boat that can't be beaten!

Have you played with remote-controlled cars before? How about boats? No? Well, try the Splash 500. This isn't just any boat. It's 70cm long and can travel up to 30km/h, which is as fast as the more expensive boats. It's made of tough plastic and it can be used on rough water as well as on calm lakes. We've got a special offer on these boats and it won't last long. You can try one out in the shop if you like. But be quick – at this price they'll sell quickly!

After you read

3 What do you think? Whole Class

- Did you change your mind after reading the text?
- Which phrases in the adverts will help sell the items most?
- Do you think everything in the adverts is true?

Go to page 75 in your Activity Book.

Key learning outcomes: read an advert for general understanding; scan an advert for specific information; talk about adverts

Text type: **an advert**

Investigate a text

1 Match the words and their definitions. Whole Class

1 quote
2 encourage
3 slogan
4 bargain

a something you buy that costs much less than usual
b some words said by another person
c to suggest that someone does something that you think would be good
d a short phrase that's easy to remember and is used to advertise something

2 Read the advert to check your answers.

a fun name for the product → **Supa Skates**

a quote from a famous person

'It's the new way to get around. You've got to try them!'
Harvey Dean, pop star

questions to raise interest → Do you find walking boring and slow?
Do you want to get to school in style?
Then Supa Skates are for you!

more description → They're extra-light and comfortable. The super-smooth wheels are built with the latest technology.

allow the reader to imagine having the product → Imagine yourself speeding past your friends in these sensational skates.

say how good the price is → And all this for the bargain price of £19.99! How could you resist?

final words to encourage people to buy → But be quick! We've only got a few pairs left.

slogan → ***Skate away today with Supa Skates!***

Discuss a text

3 Read the advert again. Answer the questions. Whole Class

1 Look at the name of the product. Which word is spelt incorrectly? Why do you think that is?
2 Is the slogan memorable? Why? / Why not?
3 Why does the advert include a quote from a famous person?
4 How many adjectives can you find? What kind of adjectives are they?

Writing skills: Writing a slogan

When we write advertising slogans, we might use alliteration and rhyme:

- **Alliteration** is when we use words with the same first letter.
- **Rhyme** is when we use words with similar sounds, usually vowel sounds.

Find the alliteration and the rhyme in: *Skate away today with Supa Skates!*

4 Look at the adverts on page 78 again. Find examples of alliteration and rhyme.

Plan and write an advert on page 76 in your Activity Book.

Key learning outcomes: identify and define key words for an advert; identify parts of an advert; write an advert; write a slogan

1 **Describe the photos. What do you think Bella is going to say about how she spends money?** Whole Class

1

2
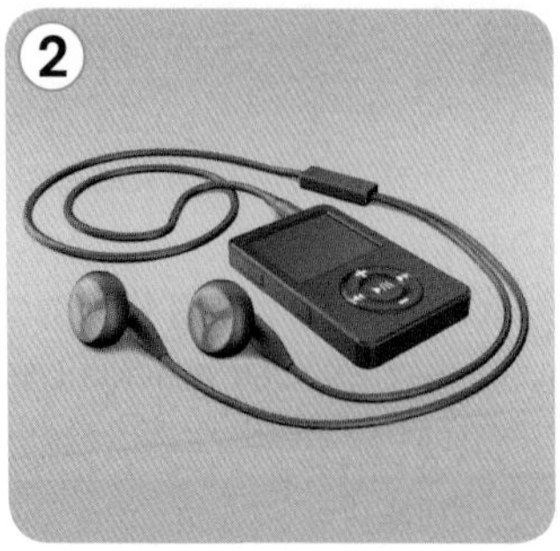

3

4

2 **Listen to the conversation. What is Bella's favourite shop? And Mark's?** CD3 25

3 **Listen again. Complete the questions below that Mark asks.** CD3 25

- Do your parents … ?
- What do you …?
- What do you … ?
- Have you … ?
- Does your family … ?

4 **Prepare a conversation about how you spend money on page 77 in your Activity Book.**

Conversation time

Remember! If you are asked a *yes / no* question, don't just say *yes* or *no*. Give some details or some examples.

Yes, I do, but I …
Yes, because …
No, because …

Go to the Song Bank, page 127.

5 **Reflect on the unit** **Read and think about your learning. What can you do now?** Whole Class

Hi there, Kelvin. All the information about the USA, money and fair trade has been fantastic. Thanks!

No problem, Jess. Let's catch up soon!

- I can talk about actions and results using *if* and *will*.
- I can find the USA on a map and talk about fair trade.
- I can read and write an advert.
- I can have a conversation about money.

Do the Unit Review on page 78 in your Activity Book.

Key learning outcomes: listen to and have a conversation about money; review learning and reflect on progress in the unit

21 CHANNEL reports

Hello. Our programme today is about some of the food in my aunt's café. Where does the food in your house come from?

1 **Watch the video. Read and say *true* or *false*. Correct the false sentences.**

1 'Banan' means 'finger' in Arabic.
2 There aren't more than 100 bananas on each banana plant.
3 They wash the bananas after they cut them.
4 The plastic keeps the bananas warm.
5 Bananas are always yellow.

2 **Watch the video again. What do the pictures show? Put them in order.**

a 
b 
c 
d 
e 

3 **Read, think and answer.** Whole Class

Thinking about buying and selling

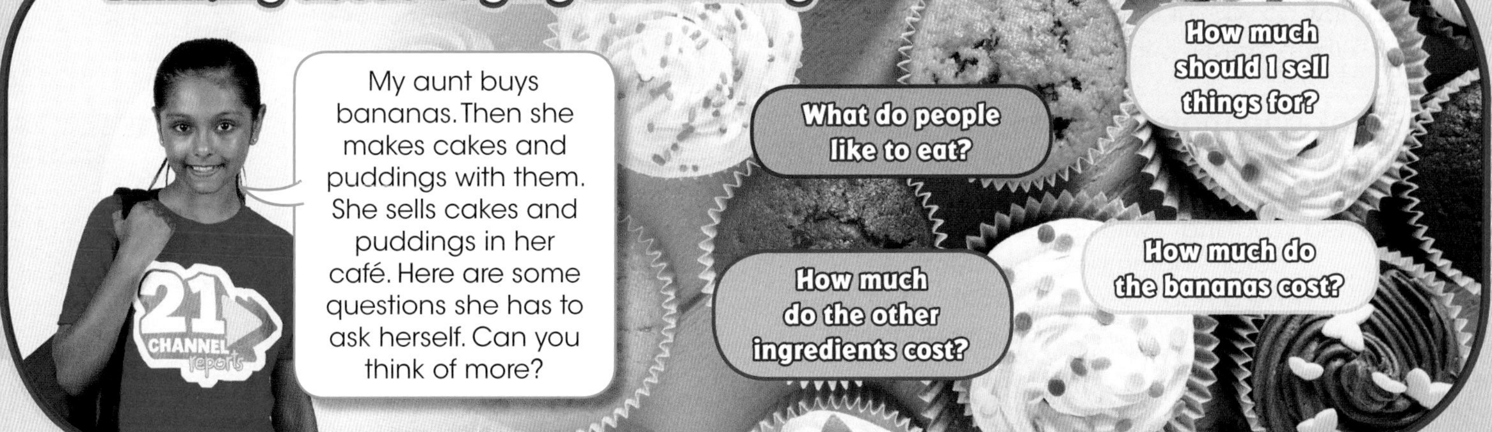

4 **Work with a partner. What could you make to sell in a café? What do you need?** Brainstorm

We could make biscuits. We need flour, butter, sugar and chocolate.

We could make smoothies. We need fruit, milk and ice cream.

Key learning outcomes: watch and understand a video about buying and selling
21st **Living in the world:** initiative and entrepeneurial skills

Unit 8 Let's dream

Objectives In this unit, I will ...

- name different things you can see and do on a tropical island.
- talk about what I'd do if I lived on a tropical island.
- learn about Ecuador and a couple who were lost near the Galapagos Islands.
- ask and answer questions about unlikely situations.
- read and write a diary extract.
- have a conversation about time travel.
- learn how to work as a team.

Look! A school in Ecuador has left a message on the project's website. I wonder how the children make a difference there.

Make a difference

Hi, everyone! My name's Eva and I live on one of the Galapagos Islands. Have you heard of them? They're part of Ecuador, but they're about 1,000km away in the middle of the Pacific Ocean. The islands are home to some very unique plants and animals. **My classmates and I are very proud of where we live, so once a month we go to a beach and pick up all the rubbish there.** Here's a photo of us in action. I'm also sending you photos of some of the amazing things that you can see and do on our islands. I hope you like them!

1 Look at Eva's photos. Answer the questions. *Whole Class*

1 What can you see in the photos?
2 How do you think the people feel?
3 Which activity is the most exciting? Why?

2 Look and match with photos 1–12. Listen, check and repeat. CD3 27

sea kayaking   wildlife spotting   palm tree
coral   hammock   giant tortoise
have a nap   sea lion   scuba diving
tropical fish   shore   boogie boarding

3 Listen and do the vocabulary quiz. CD3 28

4 Thinking skills Work with a partner. Imagine you're going to visit the Galapagos Islands. List ten things you'd take with you.

guide book   swimsuit
mosquito repellent   snorkel
binoculars

Key learning outcomes: identify and say what you can see and do on a tropical island; talk about attractions
Vocabulary: activities on a tropical island

5 **Read the rest of Eva's message. Which activity do you think is the best?**

There are lots of exciting things to do in the Galapagos Islands. My class had a vote and here are our top three favourites!

TOP THREE ATTRACTIONS

1 Visit a giant tortoise reserve Do you know that a giant tortoise is the same size as a bath? It can also weigh over 200kg and live for more than 100 years. If you want to get close to these amazing creatures, then this is the activity for you.

2 Go sea kayaking Explore the Galapagos Islands in a sea kayak. If you're lucky, you'll see sea lions, iguanas and tropical penguins swimming near the shore.

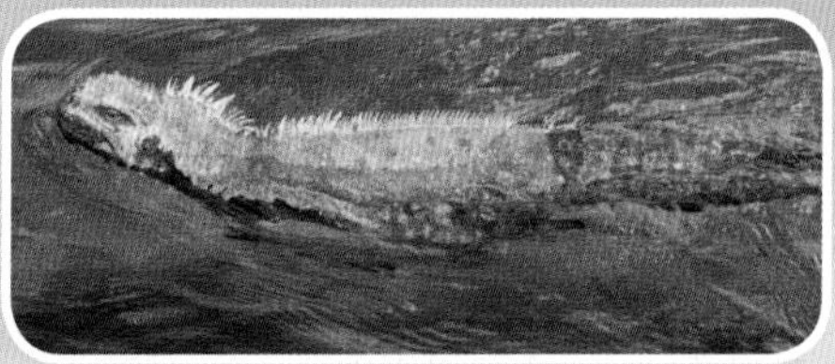

3 Hike up a volcano Have you ever wanted to climb to the top of a volcano? In this six-hour hike, you'll walk over lava fields and around the volcano's crater. The views from the top are breathtaking, but take plenty of water!

6 **Communicate** **Ask and answer about the attractions.**

Would you like to visit the giant tortoise reserve?

Yes, I would.

Why?

Because I love wildlife and I think that giant tortoises are amazing.

1 **Describe the photo. What do you think Eva did there? Read and listen to find out.** CD3 29

Hi, Eva. We all think that your project is a brilliant idea.

Thanks, Callum. Here's a photo of a beach we've cleaned recently.

Wow! It looks amazing. Do you go to the beach every day?

Not really. I prefer meeting my friends in the town centre.

Really! If I lived in the Galapagos Islands, I'd swim in the sea every day. I wouldn't go to the town centre.

☺ What else would you do?

If I lived there, I'd go sailing around the islands, too.

But the Pacific Ocean can be quite dangerous. I'll send you the link to a true story about a couple who were sailing near the islands.

What happened to them?

Ah! Read the story and see.

2 **Communicate Read and say *true* or *false*. Correct the false sentences.**

1 Callum lives in the Galapagos Islands.
2 Callum imagines living in the Galapagos Islands.
3 Callum swims in the Pacific Ocean every day.
4 Callum imagines sailing around the islands.

3 **Look and learn.**

Grammar Wall

Second conditional

If I lived in the Galapagos Islands, I would go wildlife spotting.

If I lived in the Galapagos Islands, I wouldn't climb a volcano.

We can change the order of the two halves of a conditional sentence.

I would go wildlife spotting if I lived in the Galapagos Islands.

Remember the **first conditional**:

If I go shopping, I'll buy a T-shirt.

4 **Read and think. Choose.**

Think about grammar

1 We use the first conditional to talk about something that is *probable* / *unlikely*.
2 We use the second conditional to talk about something that is *probable* / *unlikely*.

5 **Look at the dialogue in Activity 1 again. Find examples of the second conditional.**

6 **Communicate Say what you would and wouldn't do if you lived in the Galapagos Islands.**

go boogie boarding	go wildlife spotting
have a nap	go sea kayaking
climb a volcano	go scuba diving
clean a beach	go sailing

If I lived in the Galapagos Islands, I'd go boogie boarding because I love water sports.

If I lived in the Galapagos Islands, I wouldn't go boogie boarding because I'm scared of sharks.

Key learning outcomes: use the second conditional to talk about activities on a tropical island
Grammar: second conditional

Eva sent me this true story about a couple who were sailing near the Galapagos Islands.

Before you read

1 **Thinking skills** Whole Class

Read and discuss.

- What can you see in the photo on the right?
- Have you ever been sailing?
- Do you think it's an exciting activity? Why? / Why not?
- What are the dangers of sailing?

2 **Listen and read.** CD3 31

A dream trip

If you could go to New Zealand, how would you travel? In 1972, a British couple, Maurice and Maralyn Bailey, decided to sell their house and sail there in a 9.4 metre yacht called Auralyn.

Eight months later, the couple were still enjoying their adventure. However, while they were sailing towards the Galapagos Islands, their luck changed. One morning, an enormous whale smashed its tail against the side of their yacht and the yacht began sinking. The couple filled two small lifeboats with the food and equipment they needed to survive and abandoned their yacht.

At first, Maralyn and Maurice were optimistic. They expected to be rescued quickly because they were in a busy shipping lane. They also had plenty of food and water, a map, a compass, knives and a first aid kit. However, the passing ships couldn't see their tiny lifeboats and the couple soon finished all their food.

As the days passed, life became more difficult. The lifeboats were small and old and they were in danger of sinking. There were also terrible storms and giant waves overturned the lifeboats three times. To make things worse, sharks often banged the bottom of the lifeboats, looking for food.

Maurice and Maralyn were lost at sea for 117 days, drinking rainwater and eating sea turtles to survive. It was very difficult, but they encouraged each other to be positive. They told stories, made up games and planned celebrations for the future. Finally, a Korean fishing boat saw the couple. They were hungry, thirsty and sunburnt, but they were alive.

Would you ever go on a sailing trip like Maralyn and Maurice?

After you read

Go to page 82 in your Activity Book.

Values

- Was the trip a dream or a nightmare? Why?
- It's important to encourage people when things are difficult. When do you encourage your friends?
- What things do you say to encourage your friends?

Key learning outcomes: read a story with a cultural focus; listen for specific information
Values: the importance of encouraging your friends

1 Listen and read. Act out. CD3 33

Callum: The couple survived 117 days in their life boats.

Jess: That's incredible! What would you take if you had to abandon a boat?

Callum: I'd take plenty of food and water. What would you take?

Jess: Hmm … If I had to abandon a boat, I'd take a radio.

Callum: That's a good idea. You could radio for help then.

Jess: I know, but I'd be very hungry and thirsty.

Callum: Actually, I feel a bit hungry now. Let's go and get a snack!

2 Look and learn.

Grammar Wall

Second conditional questions

Would you take water **if** you abandoned a boat?

Yes, I **would**. / No, I **wouldn't**.

What **would** you do **if** you were lost at sea?

If I was lost at sea, I **would** make a sail for my boat.

3 Read and think. Choose.

Think about grammar

Which tenses do we use in second conditional questions?

1 *Would you feel* / *Do you feel* afraid if you *see* / *saw* a shark?

2 What *would you take* / *did you take* if you *go* / *went* wildlife spotting?

4 Read the story on page 85 and the dialogue in Activity 1 again. Find examples of second conditional questions.

5 Listen and read the sentences. Do you hear sentence A or B? Listen again. Repeat the sentences with the contracted form of *would*. CD3 34

Pronunciation

	A	B
1	I climb a volcano.	I'd climb a volcano.
2	They eat a pizza.	They'd eat a pizza.
3	We play the guitar.	We'd play the guitar.
4	You speak French.	You'd speak French.
5	I go to bed early.	I'd go to bed early.
6	They help me.	They'd help me.

6 Communicate Ask and answer.

visit Australia	lose your mobile phone
win some money	meet a pop star
break your leg	find a spider in your shoe

Key learning outcomes: identify contracted forms of *would*
Grammar: second conditional questions

1 Look and match. Listen, check and repeat. CD3 36

travel in space · meet a famous person · win the lottery · travel back in time · be invisible · have three wishes · get lost · be the president

1

2

3

4

5

6

7

8

2 Listen and say *A, B* or *C*. CD3 37

Listening tip!
Don't choose an answer until you have heard all of the audio.

1 If Paul travelled back in time, which period would he visit?

A

B

C

2 If Lucy met a famous person, what would she do?

A

B

C

3 Listen again. Which expressions do the children use to express uncertainty? CD3 37

- I'm not sure.
- I doubt it.
- It's very unlikely.
- You never know.
- No one knows.

4 Communicate Complete the questions in the questionnaire. Then ask and answer.

Teacher's Resource Bank: Unit 8

Key learning outcomes: identify and use language for unreal or unlikely experiences; listen for specific information; talk about unreal or unlikely situations **Vocabulary:** unreal or unlikely experiences

Before you read

1 Read and discuss. Whole Class

- Do you write a diary? What things do you write about?
- Have you ever read a book that was a diary?
- Was it fictional or was it autobiographical?
- What events did the writer describe?

2 Look at the sketches in the diary. Where do you think the writer is? Read and find out.

Reading tip!
Think about what you would expect to read in a diary extract.

Day 1
Dear Diary,
Something terrible has happened to me. I'm on a desert island and I don't know how I got here. I remember being on a ship and the sound of an explosion. Then I banged my head and I don't remember anything else. My friends were on the ship, too. I hope they're OK. I spent this morning looking for my friends. I shouted their names, but no one replied. In the afternoon, I found a bag on the shore. There was a torch, a notebook and a pen inside, but there wasn't any food. Now, it's dark and I'm scared. I've made a shelter from some palm tree leaves, but I'm hungry and thirsty. I wonder if someone will rescue me tomorrow.

Day 2
Dear Diary,
When I woke up this morning, I felt confused. I didn't want to move, but I was hungry and I needed food and water. I decided to explore the jungle. It was scary, but I found a stream with fresh water and a banana tree. While I was there, something exciting happened. A small monkey jumped on my shoulder. I couldn't believe it. I gave him some of my banana and he became my friend. I've called him Milo. Now, it's dark and I'm in the shelter on the beach again. It's cold and windy, too. I wonder if I'll find a better place to live tomorrow.

After you read

3 What do you think? Whole Class

- Is this an interesting diary?
- Which information is the most interesting?
- Would you like to change places with the writer? Why? / Why not?

Go to page 85 in your Activity Book.

Investigate a text

1 Read and answer. Whole Class

1 Look at the diary extract in Activity 2. How many days have passed since the last diary extract?
2 What have you done during this time?
3 What do you think the writer has done?

2 Read the diary extract to check your answers.

heading

Day 7
Dear Diary,
Milo and I love our cave. It's dry and the sandy floor is comfortable. We're also good at opening coconuts now. Today has been a great day. This morning, I was walking on the beach when I saw something floating in the water. It was a suitcase from the boat. I couldn't believe it! I pulled it onto the beach and quickly opened it. Inside there were some books, some clothes, a leather belt, a penknife and some glasses. I felt weak with happiness. In the afternoon, I carried the objects to the cave and afterwards I ate some bananas with Milo. I wonder what I can do with my new possessions.

chronological order

first person

detailed information

feelings

reflection

Discuss a text

3 Read the diary extract again. Find the following. Whole Class

1 when the writer wrote the diary
2 some interesting information
3 three time references
4 three different tenses
5 the writer's feelings
6 a personal reflection or thought

Writing skills: Personal pronouns and possessive adjectives

If we use the first person in a diary, the reader feels closer to us. Look at these words:

Subject pronoun	Object pronoun	Possessive adjective	Possessive pronoun
I	me	my	mine
we	us	our	ours

4 Look at all the diary extracts again. Find examples of these pronouns and adjectives.

Plan and write a diary extract for Day 10 on page 86 in your Activity Book.

1 **Describe the photos. Do they show the past, the present or the future?** Whole Class

1

2

3

2 **Listen to the conversation. What would Sam do if he could travel in time?** CD3 39

3 **Listen again. Complete the four questions that Ben asks.** CD3 39

• Would ...? • How many ...? • What ...? • What ...?

4 **Prepare a conversation about time travel on page 87 in your Activity Book.**

Conversation time

Remember! It's OK to say you're not sure if someone asks you a question.

I don't know.
I'm not sure.
Maybe.
Perhaps.

5 **Reflect on the unit** **Read and think about your learning. What can you do now?** Whole Class

Hi, Eva. Thanks for all your messages. It's been fascinating to learn about the Galapagos Islands. Say congratulations to your classmates for all their hard work cleaning the beaches.

Thanks, Callum. I will. I hope you can visit the islands one day. Speak again soon!

I can talk about what I'd do if I lived on a tropical island.

I can find the Galapagos Islands on a map and talk about a couple who were lost at sea in the Pacific Ocean.

I can read and write a diary extract.

I can have a conversation about time travel.

Do the Unit Review on page 88 in your Activity Book.

Key learning outcomes: listen to and have a conversation about time travel; review learning and reflect on progress in the unit

21 CHANNEL reports

Today's programme is about survival. What would you do if you were on a desert island?

1 **Watch the video. Read and say *true* or *false*. Correct the false sentences.**

1 You can drink rain water.
2 You only need a shelter at night.
3 The animals and plants in the rock pools are safe.
4 Some plants are poisonous.
5 A fire stops the mosquitos coming near you.

2 **Watch the video again. How can these things help you on a desert island?**

a

b

c

d

3 **Read, think and answer.** Whole Class

4 **Communicate** **Work with a partner. Do you prefer to do these tasks on your own or in a group? Why?**

do homework | do a project | study for a test | choose a present | do sport | play a computer game

I prefer doing projects in a group.

Why?

Because it's faster. We can share the work.

Key learning outcomes: watch and understand a video about desert island survival

21st **Ways of working:** working as a team

Unit 9 School: past and future

Objectives In this unit, I will ...

- name school equipment from the past and present.
- talk about what school was like in the past.
- learn about Sweden and the story of the Nobel Prizes.
- talk about my plans and predictions for school next year.
- read and write some advice for a magazine column.
- have a conversation about school.
- learn how to manage strong feelings.

Hey! We've received a message from Sweden. I can't wait to find out how the children make a difference there.

Make a difference

Hi, everyone! My name's Sven and I live in Stockholm, the capital city of Sweden. Technology is important in my country, but some elderly people don't know how to use a computer. **So my class decided to teach computer skills to the grandparents of children at school.** We meet in the school library once a week. The grandparents enjoy learning something new and we learn about life in the past. Last week, a lady told me about her school days and she gave me a photo of her old classroom. Compare it with these photos of my school now. What a big difference!

A school in the past

An Arts and Crafts lesson in my school

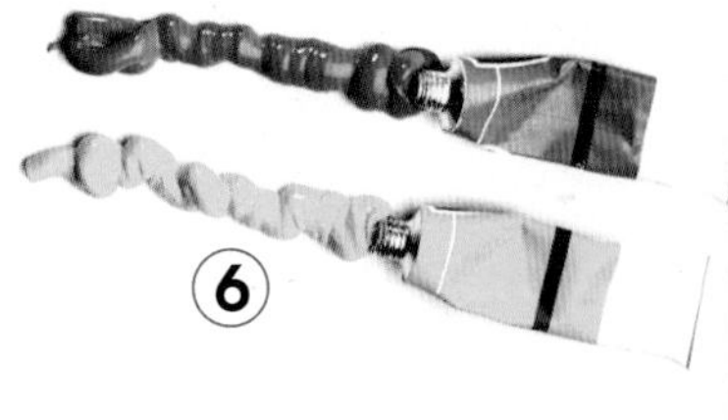

1 **Look at Sven's photos. Answer the questions.** Whole Class

1 What are the children doing?
2 Do you do these activities in your school?
3 Which activity would you like to do? Why?

2 **Look and match with photos 1–12. Listen, check and repeat.** CD3 41

canvas blackboard laptop headphones interactive whiteboard chalk overall easel rows of desks oil paints goggles laboratory

3 **Listen and do the vocabulary quiz.** CD3 42

4 **Thinking skills Copy and complete the school concept map.**

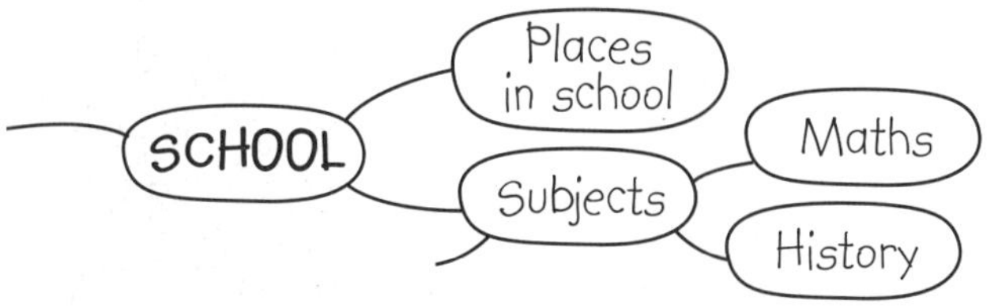

Key learning outcomes: identify and say words about school equipment from the past and present; talk about school
Vocabulary: school equipment from the past and present

A science lesson in my school

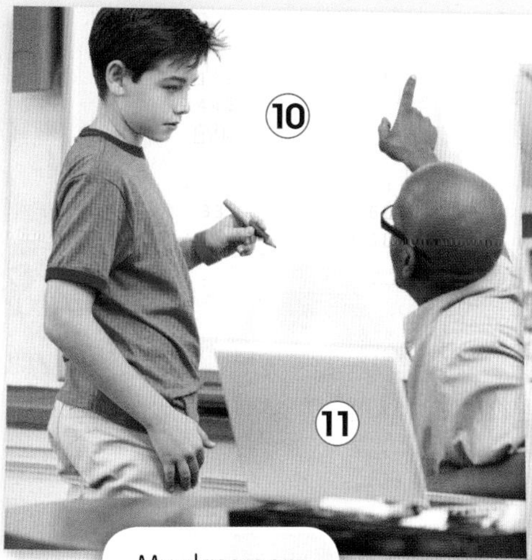

My classroom

An IT lesson

5 **Read the rest of Sven's message. Do you think this subject is a good idea? Why? / Why not?**

Do you know that some children study computer games in Swedish schools? Here's an article about a school in my city.

Time for Minecraft

Children create a virtual world when they play Minecraft.

Millions of children around the world are crazy about Minecraft, a computer game that allows players to create their own virtual world from blocks of material. A lot of children play this game in their free time, but for some lucky pupils in Stockholm, it's a school subject.

Experts believe that when the pupils play the game, they learn how to solve problems and plan for the future. Teachers at the school agree. One teacher added: 'This is an incredibly popular subject. Pupils really enjoy using their creativity to build and make objects.'

What do you think? Should all children have Minecraft classes?

6 **Communicate** **Ask and answer about school.**

What's your favourite subject at school?

Which activities do you like doing at school? Why?

Which materials do you use in this subject?

How long have you studied English at school?

1 Describe the photo. What is it? Read and listen to find out.

CD4 1

Tom: Hi, Sven. My class loved your photos and we think that the project is a great idea.

Sven: Thanks, Tom. I really enjoy listening to the grandparents talking about the past.

Tom: Was school very different when they were young?

Sven: Yes, it was. Teachers used to be a lot stricter.

Tom: And were the classrooms different, too?

Sven: Absolutely. Pupils didn't use to have laptops or calculators then.

Tom: Did they use to have books?

Sven: Yes, of course. But before they had books, pupils used to use one of these.

Tom: What is it? It looks like a tablet.

Sven: It's a slate. Pupils used to write on it with chalk.

Tom: Wow! Things have changed a lot since then.

Sven: I know. But progress is very important. I'll send you some information about important prizes for progress in Sweden.

2 Communicate Read the dialogue again. Ask and answer.

1 Does Sven like hearing about the past?
2 How were the teachers different in the past?
3 How were the classrooms different in the past?
4 Why do you think pupils used a slate in the past?

3 Look and learn.

Grammar Wall

Past habits: *used to*

I/You/He/She/We/They	used to didn't use to	study History. play computer games.

Did	I/you/he/she/we/they	use to	have the Internet?

Yes, I/you/he/she/we/they **did**.
No, I/you/he/she/we/they **didn't**.

4 Read and think. Choose.

Think about grammar

1 We use **used to** when we talk about the *present* / *past*.
2 We *can* / *can't* use **used to** when we talk about the present.

5 Look at the dialogue in Activity 1 again. Find examples of *used to*.

6 Communicate Make true sentences about schools in the past.

work in silence	sit in rows	carry rucksacks
use chalk	play basketball	
use calculators	have interactive whiteboards	

Key learning outcomes: use *used to* to talk about habits in the past
Grammar: past habits: *used to*

Before you read

Sven sent me this story about famous prizes in Sweden.

1 Thinking skills Whole Class

Read and discuss.

- Who's the person that appears on the medal?
- What things do people win a Nobel Prize for?
- Do you know any famous people who have won a Nobel Prize?

2 **Listen and read.** CD4 3

The Nobel Prizes

The Nobel Prizes are named after a Swedish scientist called Alfred Nobel. The prizes are awarded every year to people who have helped make the world a safer and better place.

1 Alfred Nobel was born in Stockholm in 1833, but when he was nine his family moved to Russia. Alfred used to spend a lot of time studying.

2 When Alfred was older, he moved back to Sweden, where he created a new explosive material.

3 Alfred became a very rich man. Then, in 1888, he had a terrible shock. A French newspaper thought that he was dead and published his obituary by mistake.

4 Alfred didn't want people to remember him like that. So he decided to change his story before it was too late.

5 Since then, many well-known people have won a Nobel Prize. These include Nelson Mandela, who fought for peace in South Africa, and Marie Curie, who discovered radium.

6 In 2014, a 17-year-old girl from Pakistan called Malala Yousafzai won the Nobel Peace Prize. Malala couldn't go to the school in her village and demanded the right for all children to receive an education.

After you read

Go to page 92 in your Activity Book.

Values

- What did Malala Yousafzai want?
- Why is it important for children to go to school?
- What other rights do children have?

Key learning outcomes: read a story with a cultural focus; listen for specific information
Values: the importance of children's rights

1 Listen and read. Act out. CD4 5

Tom: That was a really cool story. Shall we find out more about the Nobel Prizes?

Jess: OK! I'll find out about the prize ceremony.

Tom: And I'll look for information about Malala.

Later ...

Tom: What did you find out, Jess?

Jess: Well, the ceremony is held every year. The next one is going to be in December. What did you find out about Malala?

Tom: She's amazing. She's also won lots of other prizes for her work, and she's written a book.

Jess: Is she going to continue working for the rights of children?

Tom: Yes, she is. And I think she'll win many more prizes in the future.

2 Look and learn.

Grammar Wall

Future: *going to* & *will*

I'm going to have lunch at two o'clock.

I'll answer the telephone.

Remember that we use **will** for predictions, too:

I think he'll pass the exam.

3 Read and think. Complete.

Think about grammar

1 To make a future decision at the moment of speaking, we use ? + infinitive.

2 To talk about future plans, we use **to be** + ? + infinitive.

4 Look at the story on page 95 and the dialogue in Activity 1 again. Find more examples of *will* and *going to*.

5 Listen and read the sentences. What happens to the words that are underlined? Listen again and repeat. CD4 6

Pronunciation

1 I'm going to watch TV.
2 What are you going to do?
3 She's going to get married.
4 They're going to go tomorrow.
5 He's going to wash the dishes.
6 I'm going to go shopping later.

6 Communicate Ask and answer. Use *will* or *going to*.

1 What ? do at the weekend?
2 Which sports ? do in the future?
3 ? lend me some money, please?
4 Which job ? have in the future?
5 How ? travel home today?

1 Look and match. Listen, check and repeat. CD4 8

locker timetable sports kit musical instrument geometry set Physics Chemistry Literature

2 Listen and say *A, B* or *C.* CD4 9

Listening tip!
Look at the three pictures in each question. What do they show?

1 Which new subject is Anna going to study next year?

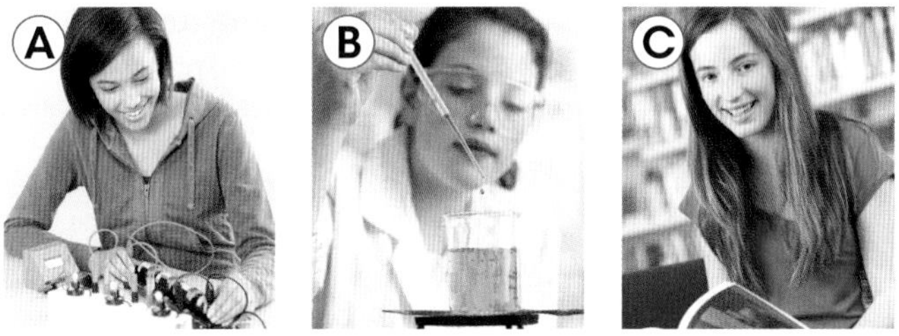

2 Where's Anna going to keep her books in secondary school?

3 Listen again. Which expressions does Anna use to say how she feels? CD4 9

- I'm nervous about …
- I'm excited about …
- I'm looking forward to …
- I'm worried about …

4 Communicate Complete the questionnaire. Then ask and answer.

Teacher's Resource Bank: Unit 9

Before you read

1 Read and discuss. Whole Class

- What things do children sometimes worry about?
- Who can children talk to about their worries?
- Have you ever read an agony aunt column in a magazine?
- Do you think these columns are a good idea? Why? / Why not?

2 Read the title and the introduction. Predict what the writer is worried about. Read and find out.

Reading tip!
Scan the text to get a general idea of the theme.

Agony Aunt

NEW SCHOOL NERVES

Are you feeling nervous about leaving primary school? Does the idea of starting secondary school stress you out? In today's column, Fran answers a message from a worried pupil in Liverpool.

Dear Fran,

I'm worried about moving to secondary school in September. Most of my friends are going to go to a different school and I know that I'm going to miss them a lot. I'm also scared that I won't make any new friends because I'm quite shy. My mum says that it's silly to worry and that I'll soon make friends, but she doesn't understand what it's like. Can you help?

Worried from Liverpool

Dear Worried from Liverpool,

Starting a new school is a big change so it's natural to worry about it. The good thing is that your new classmates will also feel nervous, so it'll be easier to make friends. Here are a few tips to help you:

- When you start your new school, try to talk to lots of people in your class.
- If you're shy, then just smile and say hi to begin with.
- If you're worried about being alone at lunchtime, you could do a lunchtime activity. You'll learn a new skill and meet pupils who've got the same interests as you.
- Finally, it's important to stay in touch with your old school friends. You can phone, text or email each other and share your experiences about life in secondary school. I'm sure it'll make you feel better.

Good luck in September!

Fran

If you're worried about something, send an email to fran@friendanonymous.com

After you read

3 What do you think? Whole Class

- Do you think it's silly to worry about making new friends?
- Do you think that Fran's advice is good?
- Which piece of advice do you think is the most useful?
- Can you think of any more advice for Worried from Liverpool?

Go to page 95 in your Activity Book.

Key learning outcomes: read an advice column for general understanding; scan an advice column for specific information; talk about advice columns

ext type: **an advice column**

Investigate a text

1 Read and discuss. Complete the sentences. Whole Class

1 When you write advice, you should sound …

friendly bossy sympathetic helpful boring

2 You should include …

suggestions rules lots of details practical ideas jokes

2 Read the advice. What do you think Messy from Manchester was worried about?

receiver's anonymous name →

Dear Messy from Manchester,

Moving to secondary school is a big step. It's natural to feel anxious because there are more books and equipment to look after. But don't worry. Here are a few tips to help you stay organised: ← opening message

advice →

- It's a good idea to pack your schoolbag the night before and check that you've got everything you need, for example your geometry set.
- It's important to read your timetable. Why don't you make a copy and stick it in your locker or on your bedroom wall? ← choices
- Make sure that you write your homework carefully in your homework diary and take your homework to school on time.
- Finally, take care of your bag and belongings during the day. Don't forget to pick up all your things at the end of each class and use your locker.

closing message → Good luck in September!

Fran

Discuss a text

3 Read the advice again. Find the following. Whole Class

1 an invented name
2 a kind comment
3 some suggestions
4 a choice
5 a practical idea
6 a positive ending to the message

Writing skills: *so* and *because*

- We use **so** to explain the <u>result</u> of something: *The secondary school is big* **so** *I'll get lost.*
- We use **because** to explain the <u>reason</u> for something: *I'll get lost* **because** *the secondary school is big.*

4 Look at the advice columns again. Find examples of *so* and *because*.

Choose a problem. Then plan and write some advice on page 96 in your Activity Book.

Key learning outcomes: identify the tone of an advice column; identify features of an advice column; write advice; use *so* and *because*

1 Look at the photos of the schools? How are they different?

Whole Class

1 nursery school

2 primary school

3 secondary school

4 university

2 Listen to the conversation. Which of these places does Lucy talk about?

CD4 11

3 Listen again. Complete the four questions that Nicole asks.

CD4 11

- What … like?
- Did …?
- Are …?
- Would …?

4 Prepare a conversation about education on page 97 in your Activity Book.

Conversation time

Remember! You can explain a word if you don't know it in English.

I don't know the word,
but it's …
a place where …
a thing that …
a person who …

Go to the Song Bank, page 127.

5 Reflect on the unit Read and think about your learning. What can you do now?

Whole Class

Hi, Sven. Thanks for all your messages. We've really enjoyed learning about your project. Have a good summer holiday!

Thanks, Tom. Have fun, too. And good luck in your new school!

I can talk about routines and habits in the past.

I can find Sweden on a map and talk about the Nobel Prizes.

I can read and write some advice for a magazine column.

I can have a conversation about school.

Do the Unit Review on page 98 in your Activity Book.

Key learning outcomes: listen to and have a conversation about school; review learning and reflect on progress in the unit

21 CHANNEL reports

Today's programme is about secondary school. Are you going to go to secondary school soon?

1 **Watch the video. Read and say *true* or *false*. Correct the false sentences.**

1 Children start secondary school when they are 12.
2 The lockers are in the classrooms.
3 Students wear goggles in the science class.
4 The girl in the video has an unhealthy lunch.
5 You make new friends in secondary school.

2 **Watch the video again. When do students use these objects?**

a 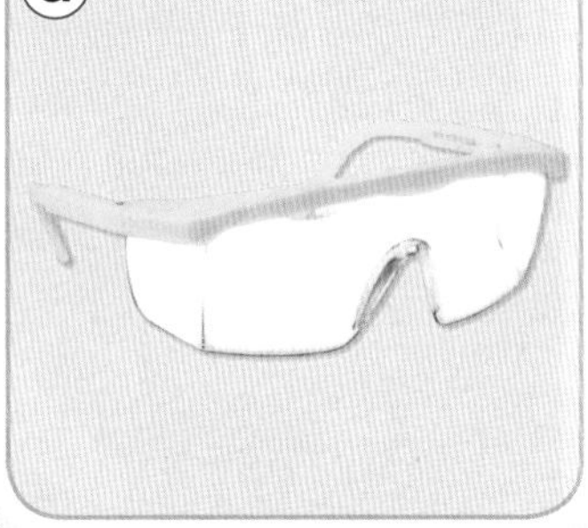

b 

c 

d 

3 **Read, think and answer.**

Managing strong feelings

It's normal to feel nervous and scared at times. Read the tips. Can you think of other tips?

Think about what is making you feel bad.

Talk about how you feel with a person you trust.

Prepare for situations that make you feel nervous or scared.

Try to be positive!

4 **Work with a partner. Are these good or bad ways of managing strong feelings?**

count to ten   shout at people   talk to a friend   write your thoughts in a diary
stay in your bedroom   do something fun

I think it's a good idea to count to ten.

I agree.

Life in the past

Research, plan and create a virtual museum about life in the past.

Share knowledge

1 **Read and discuss.** Brainstorm

- What types of museums do you know about? What is a virtual museum? What can you see and do there?
- Think about life in the past and complete the spidergram. Look at the photos to help you.

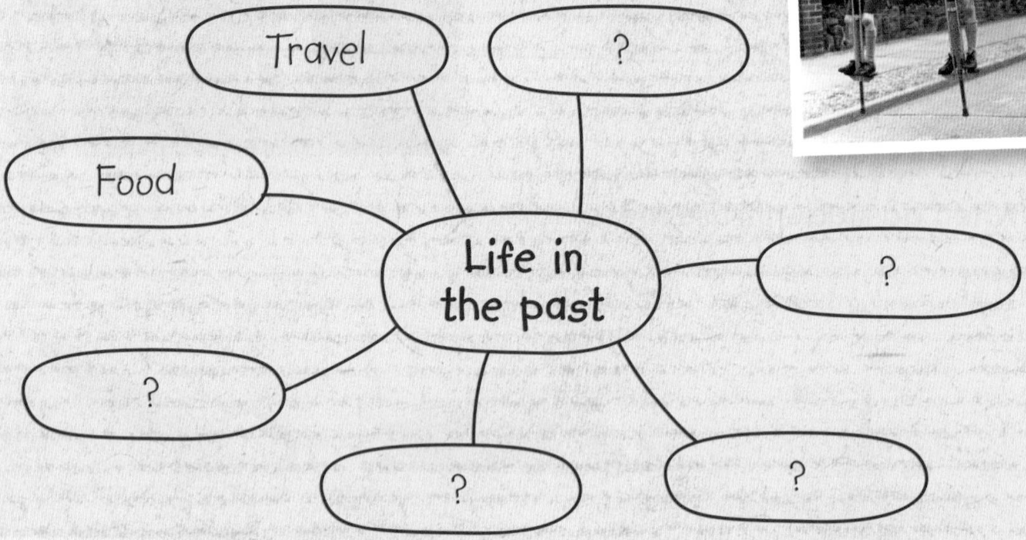

Investigate

2 **Listen to Joan's experience of life in the 1950s. Complete the notes on page 100 in your Activity Book.** CD4 13

3 **Work in a group. You're going to collect information about life in the time of your grandparents. Write questions you'd like to find the answers on page 100 in your Activity Book.** Whole Class

Cooperative learning **Make sure you listen to all members of the group before you write down the ideas.**

4 **Now find answers to the questions. Ask elderly friends and relatives or use the Internet. Take notes of the answers. Take photos of old objects or find pictures on the Internet for your virtual museum. You can record audio files, too.** ICT

Key learning outcomes: share knowledge about life in the past; write questions about the past
Language: life in the past

Plan and create your project

1 **Share the information you have with your group. Choose the topic you'd like to include in the virtual museum. Find an object to put in the museum, too. Write the information on page 101 in your Activity Book.** Whole Class

1 Which topic are you presenting?
2 Why have you chosen it?
3 What is interesting about it?
4 How much information did you find out about it?

Language bank

What did she say about (life at school)?
She said she (sat at the same desk every day).
Let's do our project about (school in the past).

2 **Prepare your information for the virtual museum.**

Steps:

1. Choose a topic for your project.
2. What's the best way of presenting the information to the class? Will you draw some of the information or write about it? Have you got photos you could show or objects you could bring in?
3. What tasks do you need to do? Who's going to do each task?
4. What materials do you need and where will you get them from?

Project tip!

You can keep a museum of objects in your classroom, too. Make information labels for the objects.

Cooperative learning **Make sure that you split the tasks equally and that each person in the team has a similar amount to do.**

Present your project

3 **Present your virtual museum to the class. Take turns to answer any questions.**

Read and answer the questions on page 101 in your Activity Book.

Key learning outcomes: work in a group to plan a virtual museum; present your virtual museum to the class
Language: talking about habits in the past: *Children used to (listen to radio programmes) ...*

Thanksgiving Day

4th Thursday in November

1 **What's the weather like in November in your country? What season is it? Read and find out about a November festival in the USA.** Whole Class

In autumn, on the fourth Thursday in November, people in the USA celebrate Thanksgiving Day. There is a long weekend holiday of four or five days for schools, and people often travel a long way to be with their family and friends. People have a special meal together.

The first Thanksgiving meals happened in the 17th century. This was when the first people travelled from England to live in America. Each year they planted seeds and grew food. In November they had a big meal to celebrate that they had enough food.

Today, many other events happen during that weekend too. In some big cities there are parades on the streets. New York has had a Thanksgiving Parade since 1924. There are school marching bands and many huge balloons of cartoon characters. Sport is also an important part of the Thanksgiving celebrations. There are many American football games. The Detroit Lions have played a game at their stadium on every Thanksgiving Day since 1945.

2 **Read the text again. Answer the questions.**

1 What is the date of Thanksgiving Day this year?
2 When did people travel to America from England for the first time?
3 Why did they celebrate each year?
4 Which has happened more often: the Thanksgiving Parade in New York or the Thanksgiving Day game in Detroit?

3 **What is the most important meal in the year for your family? What do you eat? Read about the Thanksgiving meal. Match the red words with the letters.**

The turkey is the most common main meal. Some people call Thanksgiving 'Turkey Day'. The turkey usually has stuffing inside it. The stuffing is a mixture of bread and vegetables and sometimes has apple, too.

With the turkey, some people serve an orange vegetable, called squash. They cook it with sugar and they put sweet marshmallows on the top, too.

A typical dessert is a warm sweet pie. This one is made with apples and has got pecan nuts on the top.

4 **Read and listen to the poem. Write your own poem. Use a word about Thanksgiving Day.** CD4 14

Digital tip!

Use the Internet to find out about Thanksgiving festivals in other countries. What do people in those countries do? ICT

Thanksgiving

Thanksgiving Day is coming soon
Under orange leaves of autumn.
Remember what it's all about
Kindness, happiness and fun.
Every year we invite our friends
You can come too if you want!

Endangered Species Day

3rd Friday in May

1 What does 'endangered species' mean? Read and find out.

Every year, on the third Friday in May, people remember the importance of protecting endangered species. These are animals and plants that are in danger of disappearing completely from the world. If this happened, these species would become extinct. Humans are often responsible for this. They sometimes destroy an animal's habitat when they cut down trees, block rivers or build new houses. They pollute water, which can affect many fish and birds. Some animals are hunted for their meat and fur. Climate change is also affecting where animals live. It can change the temperature and make it difficult for some species to survive.

Endangered Species Day began in the USA. On this day, thousands of people visit zoos, botanical gardens, aquariums and wildlife refuges to learn more about how we can help protect endangered species.

2 Read the text again. Answer the questions.

1 What date is Endangered Species Day this year?
2 How do humans put the lives of animals and plants in danger?
3 What happens on Endangered Species Day?
4 What's the word that means that a species has disappeared?

3 Look at the photos. What animals are mentioned? Can you think of any reasons why these animals might be endangered? Read and find out.

Polar bears

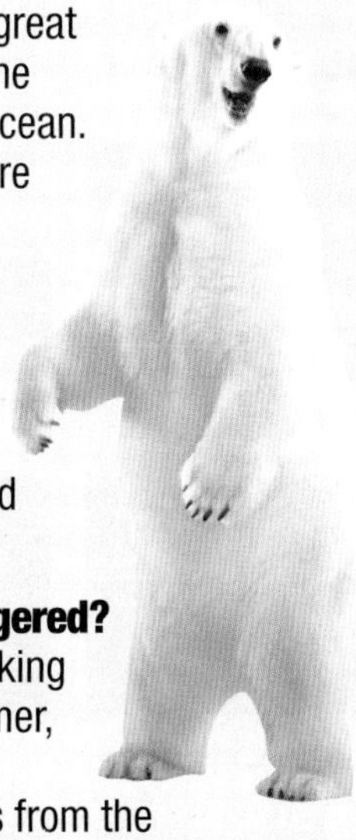

Facts: They spend a great part of their lives on the sea ice in the Arctic Ocean. It's estimated that there are between 20,000 and 25,000 left.

Why are they important?
They're an important part of the marine food chain.

Why are they endangered?
Climate change is making the Arctic Ocean warmer, so the ice is melting. Polar bears hunt seals from the sea ice, so they need the sea ice to survive.

Vaquitas

Facts: They live in the sea near Mexico. They can be up to 1.5 metres long. There are fewer than 200 left.

Why are they important?
Of all the mammals in the sea, vaquitas are most in danger. If they aren't protected, they'll become extinct.

Why are they endangered?
They're accidentally caught in fishing nets from fishing boats.

Orang-utans

Facts: They live in Indonesia and Malaysia. There are under 50,000 in the world, but there were more than 200,000 a hundred years ago. Female orang-utans only give birth every three to five years, so it's difficult for the population to grow.

Why are they important?
They help disperse seeds in the forest, so they play an important role in preserving their habitat.

Why are they endangered?
Sometimes they're hunted and kept as pets. Also, their habitats are disappearing because humans are cutting down trees in the forest.

4 Listen and say the animal from Activity 3. CD4 15

Digital tip!
Use the Internet to find out about Endangered Species Day last year. What events took place? ICT

Grammar

1 Past simple & past continuous with *while*

While	I he she	was	painting,	it started raining.
	you we they	were		

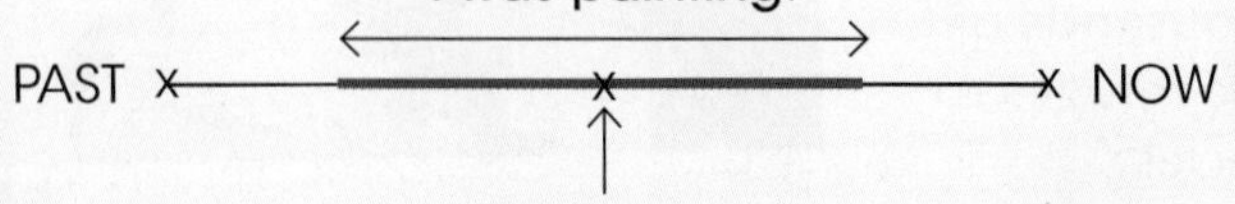

We use the past simple with the past continuous when one action interrupts another action in the past. Remember that we put **while** before the action that began first (in the past continuous).

2 Verbs that are followed by the infinitive or the gerund

He agreed	to push	the trolley.
He likes	travelling	by plane.

Verb + infinitive	Verb + gerund
agree	like
decide	enjoy
try	start
promise	stop
want	imagine
learn	suggest

Some verbs are followed by the **infinitive** form of the verb. Some verbs are followed by the **gerund** form of the verb. You need to learn which verbs are followed by the infinitive and which verbs are followed by the gerund.

Vocabulary

1 Air travel

arrivals

departures

queue

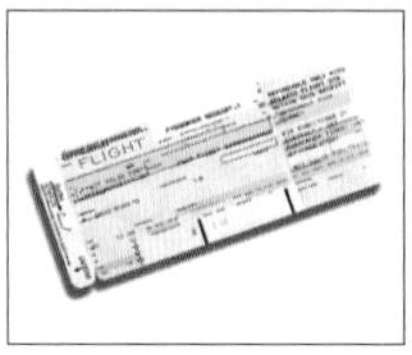

boarding pass

hand luggage

passenger

check-in desk

trolley

take off

flight attendant

land

runway

2 Travel and tourism

guard

backpacker

platform

ticket office

receptionist

reception

guest

tourist information centre

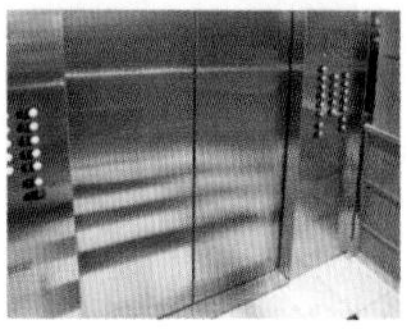
lift

Practise in your Activity Book (page 102).

Grammar

1 Present perfect questions

Have	I/you/we/they	ever	been sailing?
Has	he/she		played rugby?

Yes/No,	I/you/we/they	have/haven't.
Yes/No,	he/she	has/hasn't.

We use the present perfect to talk about an experience.

2 Past simple questions

When	did	I/you/he/she/we/they	go sailing?

We use the past simple to talk about specific details of an experience.

3 Present perfect: *for* & *since*

How long	have	I/you/we/they	done gymnastics?
	has	he/she	sung in a choir?

I/You/We/They	have	done gymnastics	for two years.
He/She	has	sung in a choir	since last year.

We use **for** to talk about the period of time.
We use **since** to say when the action started.

for two months / since September

PAST ——x——————→ NOW

September October November

We use the present perfect with **for** and **since** to talk about actions that began in the past and continue to the present.

For	Since
half an hour	one o'clock
one day	break time
five years	5th September

Vocabulary

1 Sports and equipment

fencing

trampolining

archery

hoop

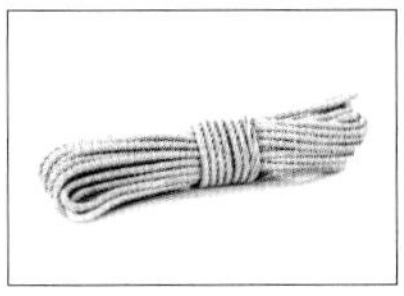
rope

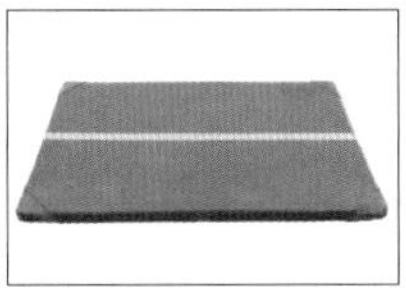
crash mat

gymnastics

athletics

martial arts

net

racket

water polo

2 Hobbies

sing in a choir

go to drama class

belong to a sports club

do circus skills

do photography

do needlework

make models

collect cards

Practise in your Activity Book (page 103).

Grammar

1 Countable nouns: *too* & *enough*

There	are	too many	onions in this salad.
There	aren't	enough	tomatoes.

Other expressions of quantity for countable nouns: **some, a few, lots of, a lot of, not many, not any**

2 Uncountable nouns: *too* & *enough*

There	is	too much	garlic in this dish.
There	isn't	enough	rice.

Other expressions of quantity for uncountable nouns: **some, a little, lots of, a lot of, not much, not any**

Some food can be countable or uncountable.
1 There's **some chocolate** in the fridge. (uncountable, part of a chocolate bar)
2 There are three **chocolates** in the box. (countable, individual chocolates)

3 Modal verbs for necessity: *need to, don't need to, needn't*

I/You/He/She/We/They	need to	eat more fruit.
	needn't don't need to	jog every day.

When something is necessary, we use **need to**. When something isn't necessary, we use **needn't** or **don't need to**.

4 Modal verbs for obligation, prohibition and advice

Obligation
You must eat fruit and vegetables every day.

Prohibition
You mustn't drink too many fizzy drinks.

Advice
You should do regular exercise.
You shouldn't watch too much TV.

Vocabulary

1 Food

an avocado

an onion

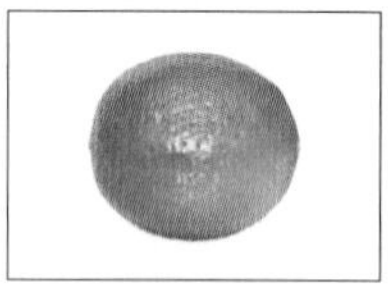
a lime

a chilli pepper

prawns

corn

turkey

beans

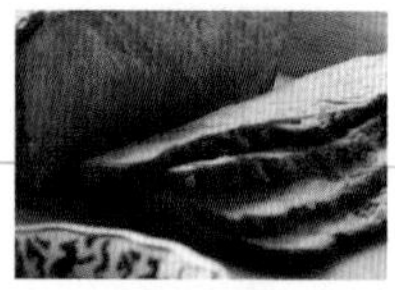
beef

cinnamon

garlic

peanuts

2 Keeping fit and healthy

do exercise

eat junk food

go for walks

drink fizzy drinks

eat fruit and vegetables

drink water

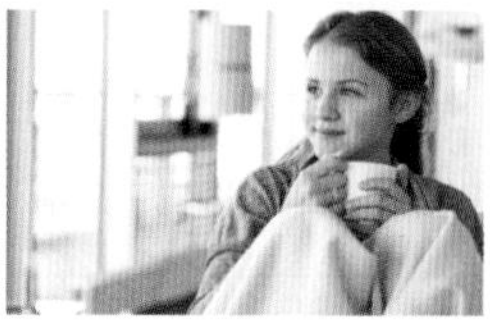
rest

spend time on the computer

Practise in your Activity Book (page 104).

Grammar

1 Past passive

The film	was made wasn't made	by Disney Pixar. by DreamWorks.
The songs	were sung weren't sung	by The Beatles. by Lady Gaga.

To form a passive sentence in the past, we use the past simple of the verb **to be** and the past participle of the verb. We need to use **by** when we say who did the action.

2 Past participles

Regular

Infinitive	Past simple	Past participle
compose	composed	composed
design	designed	designed
perform	performed	performed

Irregular

Infinitive	Past simple	Past participle
write	wrote	written
sing	sang	sung
build	built	built
make	made	made

3 Past passive questions

When The Eiffel Tower	was was built	the Eiffel Tower built? in 1889.
Where Guernica	was was painted	Guernica painted? in France.
Who The books	were were written	the books written by? by J.K.Rowling.

Remember that we need to use **was** for a single object and **were** for more than one object.

Vocabulary

1 Creative activities

puppet

do origami

do ceramics

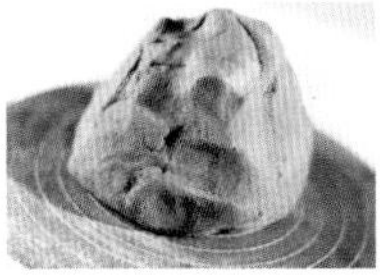
clay

perform a play

costume

stage

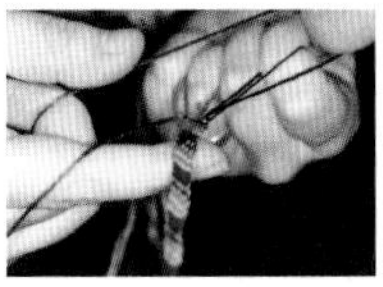
make jewellery

beads

make a film

create an animation

do traditional dancing

2 Artistic professions

composer

novelist

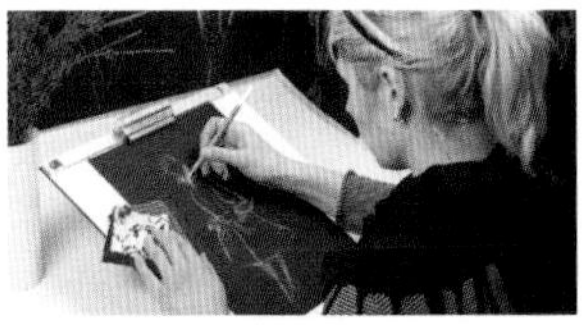
fashion designer

photographer

actor

sound engineer

graffiti artist

film director

Practise in your Activity Book (page 105).

Grammar

1 Reported speech

The news **is** interesting.

He said He told me	the news	**was** interesting.

I **like** reading comics.

He said He told me	he	liked reading comics.

I'**m reading** the newspaper.

She said She told me	she	**was** reading the newspaper.

When we report what people say, we need to change the tense. The present simple usually changes to the past simple.

2 Reported speech: *will* / *would* & *can* / *could*

My team **will** win.

She said She told me	her team	**would** win.

My little sister **can't** read yet.

He said He told me	his little sister	**couldn't** read yet.

When we report what people say, **will** changes to **would** and **can** changes to **could**.

Vocabulary

1 Messages and communication

advert

text message

greetings card

brochure

sign language

cartoon

sign

blog post

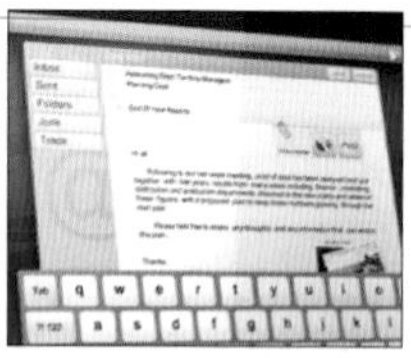
email

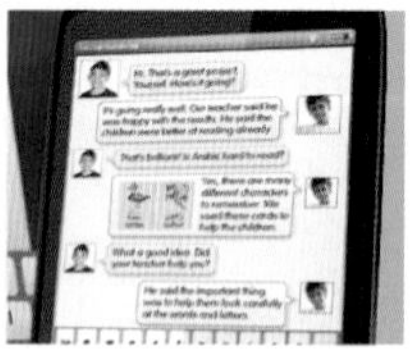
chat message

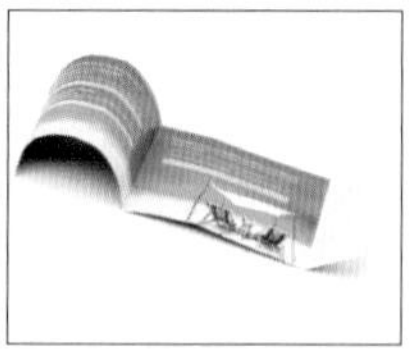
leaflet

note

2 News features

front page

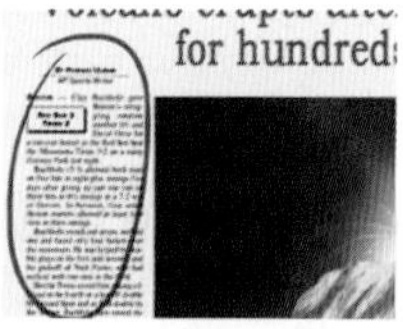
article

headline

interview

reporter

review

fashion section

world news

sports news

caption

Practise in your Activity Book (page 106).

Grammar

1 Making predictions about the future: modal verbs

I	will finish	my homework today.	(certain)
I	may be might be could be	a politician.	(possible)
I	won't go	skiing this winter.	(certain)

Remember that modal verbs are always followed by the infinitive form of the verb.

2 Making predictions about the future: modal verbs with adverbs

I	will	definitely probably	win the race.	(more certain) (less certain)
I	definitely probably		won't win the race.	(more certain) (less certain)

We can use the adverbs **definitely** and **probably** to say if we're more or less certain of something.

3 Embedded questions

Direct question

Will you be famous in the future?

Embedded question

Do you think you'll be famous in the future?

Do you know that embedded questions sound more polite than direct questions in English?

4 Future time references

soon
later
this afternoon
tonight
tomorrow evening
the day after tomorrow
next week
in one day's time
in ten minutes' time
in the future

Vocabulary

1 Jobs

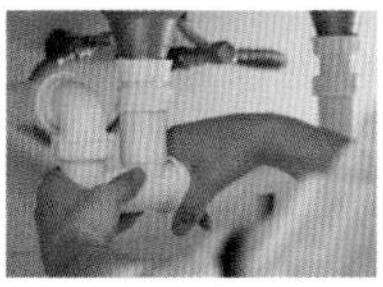

plumber

security guard

politician

electrician

tour guide

archaeologist

veterinary nurse

computer technician

graphic designer

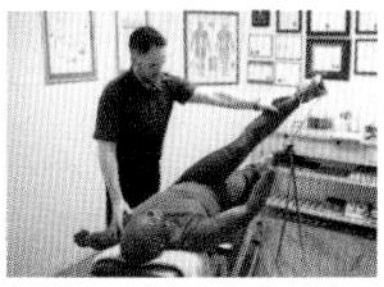

physiotherapist

businessperson

detective

2 Life events

have children

get a job

leave home

go to university

learn to drive

go backpacking

get married

start a business

Practise in your Activity Book (page 107).

Grammar

1 Comparative and superlative adjectives: regular & irregular

Adjective	Comparative	Superlative
big	bigger	the biggest
large	larger	the largest
shiny	shinier	the shiniest
expensive	more expensive	the most expensive
good	better	the best
bad	worse	the worst
far	farther/further	the farthest/furthest

2 Comparative forms: *too* & *not enough*

He's too young / not old enough to play the game.

3 Comparative forms: *(not) as … as*

The car is **more** expensive **than** the bicycle.
The bicycle is **not as** expensive **as** the car.

The blue car is **as** expensive **as** the red car.

4 First conditional

If you compare prices, you'll save money.

If she **doesn't** compare prices, she **won't** save money.

What **will** happen **if** they compare prices?

Remember that we use the first conditional to talk about the result of a possible action in the future. The sentence half that includes **if** uses a verb in the present simple. The other half of the sentence uses the future with **will**.

Vocabulary

1 Money and shopping

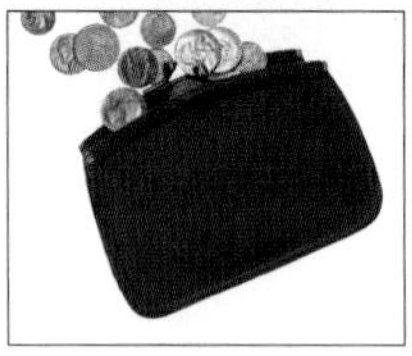
purse

credit card

coins

banknotes

price tag

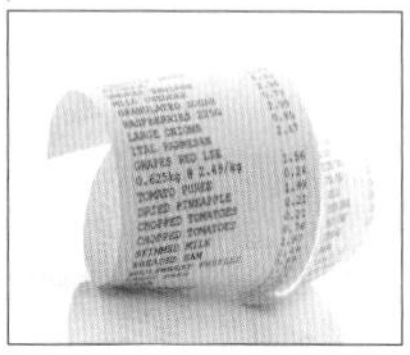
receipt

customer

cashier

till

spend money

save money

moneybox

2 Describing damaged objects

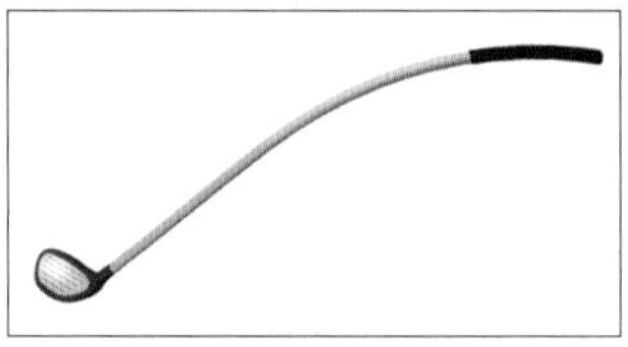
bent

cracked

faulty

loose

ripped

scratched

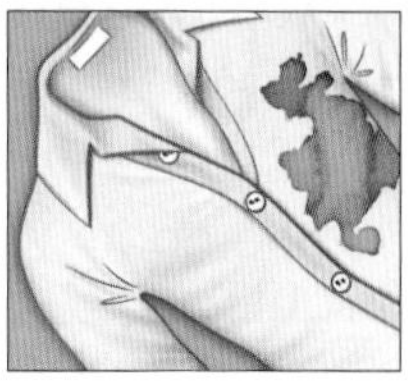
stained

Practise in your Activity Book (page 108).

Grammar

1 Second conditional

If I lived on a tropical island, I **would** go snorkelling every weekend.
If I won the lottery, I **wouldn't** buy a boat.

I **would** take some water if I climbed a volcano.
I **wouldn't** feel afraid if I saw a giant tortoise.

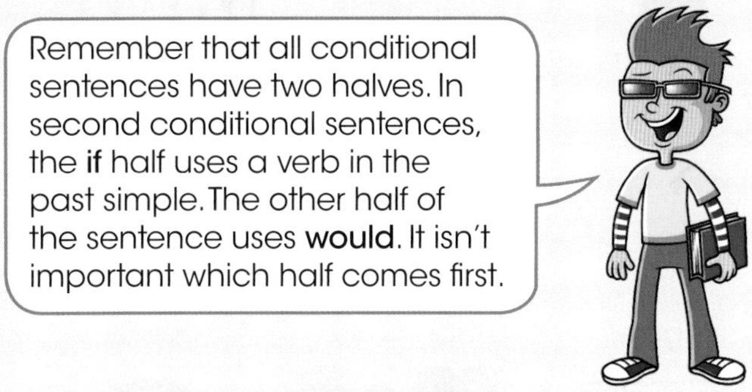

2 Second conditional questions

What **would** you do if you met a famous actor?
Where **would** you go if you won the lottery?
What **would** you say if you saw a bear?

Would you be scared if you saw a shark?
Yes, I **would**. / No, I **wouldn't**.

Vocabulary

1 Activities on a tropical island

scuba diving

tropical fish

coral

have a nap

palm tree

hammock

wildlife spotting

giant tortoise

boogie boarding

sea kayaking

sea lion

shore

2 Unreal or unlikely experiences

win the lottery

get lost

travel back in time

be invisible

be the president

travel in space

meet a famous person

have three wishes

Practise in your Activity Book (page 109).

Grammar

1 Past habits: *used to*

I/He/She/ You/We/They	used to	use a slate.
	didn't use to	use a computer.

Did	I/he/she/ you/we/ they	use to	have rows of desks?

Yes, I/you/he/she/we/they **did**.
No, I/you/he/she/we/they **didn't**.

2 Future: *going to* & *will*

I	am	going to	do my homework this evening.
He She	is	going to	watch TV tonight.
You We They	are	going to	go to the beach.

I	will	open the window.
		tidy up the classroom.

Vocabulary

1 School equipment

chalk

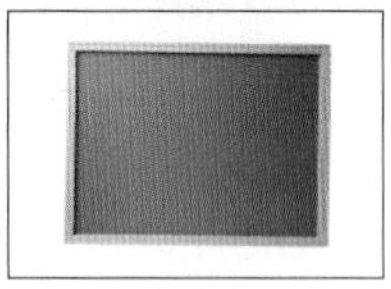
blackboard

rows of desks

easel

canvas

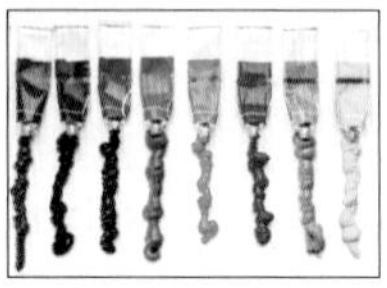
oil paints

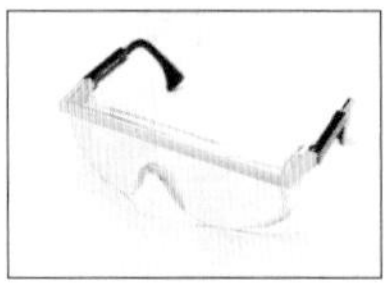
goggles

laboratory

overall

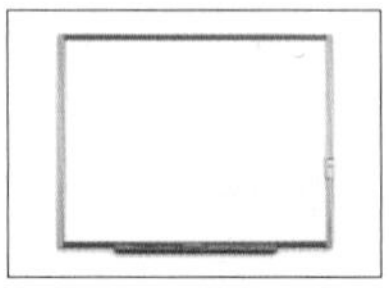
interactive whiteboard

laptop

headphones

2 Secondary school

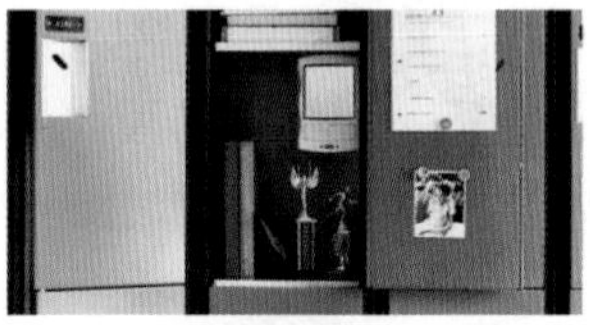
locker

sports kit

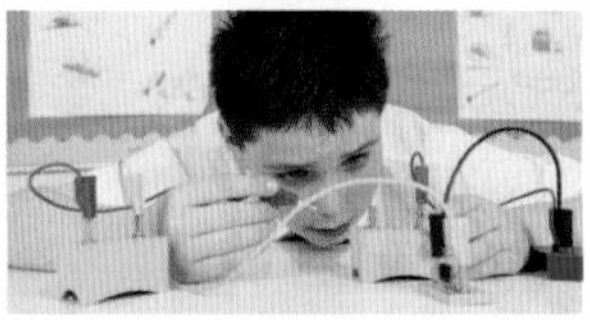
Physics

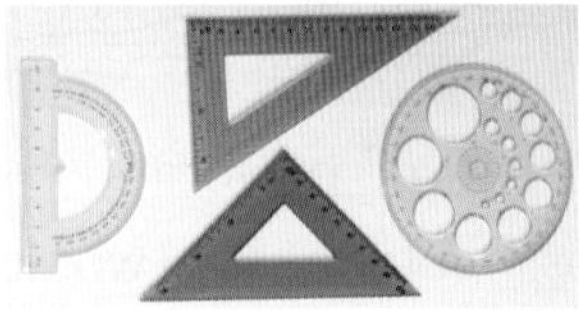
geometry set

Chemistry

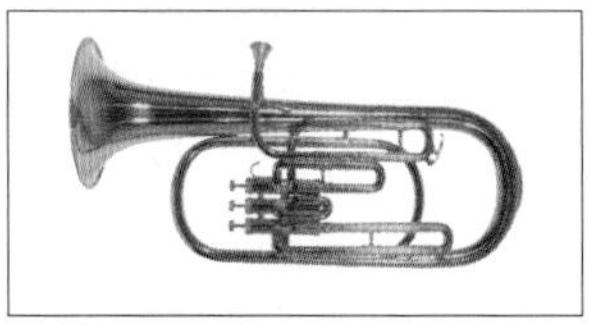
musical instrument

Literature

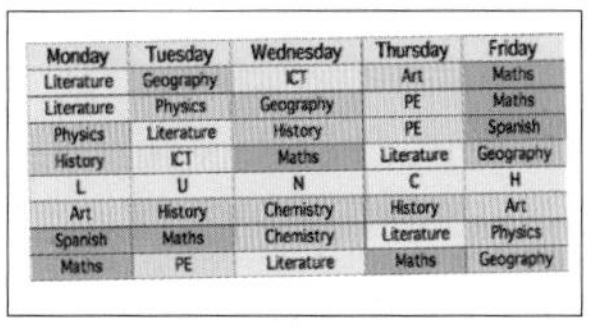

Monday	Tuesday	Wednesday	Thursday	Friday
Literature	Geography	ICT	Art	Maths
Literature	Physics	Geography	PE	Maths
Physics	Literature	History	PE	Spanish
History	ICT	Maths	Literature	Geography
L	U	N	C	H
Art	History	Chemistry	History	Art
Spanish	Maths	Chemistry	Literature	Physics
Maths	PE	Literature	Maths	Geography

timetable

Practise in your Activity Book (page 110).

1 **Read the sign. Where do you think it is? Who do you think it is for?**

2 **Read the sentences about the sign. Which one is true? Which words in the sign helped you?**

1 Everyone must call this phone number.
2 People who saw the accident must call this phone number.
3 People must call this phone number at 3pm.

3 **Read the short texts. What kind of texts are they and who are they for? Choose the correct answer for each one.**

①

Dear Mum and Dad,

We're having a great time on the school trip. We couldn't go on the boat trip because it was raining, but we had fun at the transport museum. We'll go on the boat trip tomorrow if the weather is good.

See you next week!

Ellie

A Ellie has already been on a boat trip.
B Ellie is going on a boat trip tomorrow.
C Ellie may go on the boat trip tomorrow.

A You have to check in at least 30 minutes before your flight.
B The check-in for all international flights will close in 30 minutes.
C Don't check in more than 30 minutes before your flight.

A You can use the stairs or the lift.
B Another lift is through the door.
C You must use the stairs to go up.

4 **Can you think of other times when people need to write a very short text?**

Exam help — Learning to learn

Q: What do I do if I think two answers are correct?
A: Don't worry! Read the text again and check which one matches what the text says.

1 Read the text quickly. Then answer the questions.

Whole Class

1 What kind of text is it?
an advertisement   a website   a biography

2 What is the writer trying to do?
explain the rules of fencing   describe her experiences   advertise her club

FENCING

by Imogen Ross, aged 13

Many of my friends think it's unusual, but I really like doing a sport that is different. They all do dance or play football and netball. I love fencing. I started when I was 8 and I haven't looked back since!

I'd really recommend it as a sport for young people. It's great exercise for your arms and your legs. You have to move forwards and backwards quickly and be really accurate with your arm movements. What I find the most difficult is the concentration. You have to think carefully about every move. What might your opponent do and how are you going to defend yourself? Then you have to act quickly. I think it's similar to chess – but faster!

People often ask me how I started. It was just luck. I was with my dad at the sports centre and a woman was walking around asking if any children wanted to have a free fencing lesson. My dad's always been interested in fencing. He says that my grandad was a good fencer. Anyway, he persuaded me to try it.

I've made a lot of friends since I joined the club. It's an individual sport, but we all support each other when we play. We give each other advice too. Sometimes it's easier for someone watching you to see what you are doing wrong.

Competitions are fun but they're very tiring, so I don't do too many of them. The competitions are sometimes quite far away so we need to get up early and get home late. I haven't won anything yet, but I've come second and third a few times.

2 Read the text again and answer the questions. For each question, choose A, B, C or D.

1 Fencing is similar to chess because
A they can both be played quickly.
B you have to use your arms.
C you have to predict your opponent's moves.
D you take turns to move.

2 Imogen started fencing because
A a person at the sports centre invited her to try it.
B her grandad talked to her about it.
C her dad was helping with the training.
D she saw a notice and decided to try it.

3 What does Imogen think about people giving her advice?
A It's good, but not during competitions.
B It makes her feel part of a team.
C She doesn't like people saying what is wrong.
D It's helpful because she can't see all her mistakes.

4 Which of these would Imogen say to a friend?
A Fencing is a dangerous sport.
B Fencing is a fun and sociable sport.
C Fencing is a very competitive sport.
D Fencing isn't good for getting fit.

Exam help

Learning to learn

Q: Where can I find the information to answer the questions?

A: It depends. Sometimes you need to look for a fact in one part of the text. At other times you need to think about the whole text.

Reading

1 Read and correct the mistakes.

1 This is one my favourite restaurants.

2 There are always too much people in the evening.

3 The best time to visit is at about 6.00 the afternoon.

4 In the evening, you need reserve a table.

5 I order a milkshake ever time I visit.

6 I haven't been there since two months.

2 Read the email with the missing words. Answer the questions.

From: To:

Subject:

Hi Jason,

I've invited (1) few friends to come with my family for a birthday lunch. We (2) going to Burritos, the new Mexican restaurant. (3) you like Mexican food?

We're going on Sunday. The table is reserved for 1pm. Can we (4) there at 12.45pm? After the meal, we will go to the park (5) the weather is good. My dad can take you home by car at about 3.30.

I've attached the restaurant menu. All of the food is delicious. We are choosing tomato salad, beef burritos and cheesecake. Is that OK (6) you?

John is bringing his sister. Does your sister, Mia, want (7) come too?

Could your parents call my dad? His mobile is 0718766.
Hope to see you there!
Ben

1 Which day are they going to the restaurant?
2 What vegetable are they going to eat?
3 What is the name of Jason's sister?

3 Write the seven missing words in your notebook. Compare with a friend. Try to explain why you chose each word.

4 Write sentences with missing words. Test your friend.

Exam help — Learning to learn

Q: What are the important things to check when I have finished?

A: You need to write the words correctly so check your spelling carefully. It's a good idea to read through all of the text. Do the sentences with your words sound right?

1 **Read and discuss. How are these words different?** Whole Class

A concert B musical C play D exhibition

2 **Read the text with the missing words. What do you learn about stage schools?**

Life at a stage school

Twelve-year-old Mark goes to a stage school in London. In the morning, the school (1) like any other school. All the students have to wear a smart uniform and they study normal school subjects like Maths and Science. However, in the afternoon, the children have theatre classes where they learn (2) to sing, dance and act. It's hard (3), but everyone agrees that it's the best part of the day.

Just like the other children in his class, Mark (4) to the theatre school because he wants to be a professional performer. He has already performed in a musical where he had to sing and dance. However, he is more (5) in acting. 'My ambition is to appear in a film,' he says. 'I love watching comedies and action films so it would be amazing to be in one.' With all Mark's hard work and talent, we're certain that his (6) will come true.

3 **Read the text again. Choose the correct word for each space.**

1	A sounds	B looks	C feels	D smells
2	A how	B what	C where	D when
3	A job	B work	C business	D occupation
4	A goes	B arrives	C joins	D brings
5	A excited	B interested	C keen	D good
6	A thought	B idea	C dream	D hope

4 **Read the text a third time. Does the completed text make sense?**

Exam help Learning to learn

Q: What do I do if I'm not sure what the missing word is?

A: Don't panic. Read the four choices again. Think about how the words are different.

Reading

1 Read about these four teenagers. Then answer the questions.

Alice is interested in how things work. She likes taking mechanical things apart and putting them back together. She'd like to find out more about engines, but she isn't interested in old things.

Karim likes sport, especially swimming. He likes being active. He also likes teaching younger children to do things. He only likes teaching sport, though. He's also interested in healthy eating.

Ben does a lot of writing. He keeps his own blog about music that he likes. He doesn't play any instruments himself, though. He also likes reading and writing about current affairs.

Ella likes art and draws a lot, but she doesn't want a job as an artist. She's interested in films and likes films set in the past. She wants to find out more about what people do on a film set.

1 What isn't Alice interested in?
2 What does Ben like writing about?
3 What does Karim like teaching?
4 What does Ella want to find out about?

2 The teenagers are going to do some work experience this summer. Read and decide which place would be most suitable for each teenager. There will be one place left over.

A CENTRAL LEISURE CENTRE
We'll show you how we prepare all areas of the leisure centre, including the pool. You'll help keep the centre clean, serve customers and set up the sports equipment. We'd like you to assist the teachers in the swimming pool, too.

B History of Science Museum
Are you interested in telescopes and microscopes that were made more than 150 years ago? Then we need your help to organise an exhibition of these machines. You'll be helping people around the museum and in our café, too. It's ideal if you like science.

C ABC Media
We're a small company who make all kinds of films, from music videos and sports videos to educational films. You would work with the producer and see how we direct the actors and how we edit the films.

D Stanton Echo Newspaper
If you want to be a journalist, this is for you. You'll spend each day with a different editor or designer from the news, sports or entertainment departments. We'll let you write and edit some short newspaper articles, too.

E STANTON AERODROME
You won't be flying any planes! This experience is about helping in the mechanics department where we repair the engines. You need to have an interest in engineering and need to be happy getting your hands dirty!

3 Write a few sentences about the kind of person who would be suitable for the other place.

Exam help Learning to learn

Q: There's so much text to read! Where do I start?

A: In this task, it's best to start with the descriptions of the four people. It's useful to underline one or two important details in each description.

1 **Read the title and predict what the text is about.** Whole Class

2 **Quickly read the text to find out. Then answer the questions.**

1 Which paragraph describes the transport?
2 Which paragraph describes the entertainment?
3 Which paragraph explains a special offer?
4 Which paragraph describes the accommodation?

Amazing space holiday offer

Summer 2030

Are you tired of lying on a crowded beach every summer? (1) Take advantage of our special offer and book an amazing space holiday today.

Your holiday begins with a relaxing trip in a modern space shuttle. You can depart from one of five different spaceports around the world. (2) That's enough time to sit back, eat a snack and enjoy the incredible sight of Earth from space.

Once the shuttle has arrived, you are free to enjoy the excellent facilities in our five-star hotel. (3) Each one has got a private bathroom, a fridge and internet connection. Dinner is in our famous *Space Eye* restaurant. It offers a wide variety of delicious food. (4)

There are activities to keep everyone entertained. There is a library, a cinema and a science lab where you can help with the experiments. (5) They can choose from a selection of zero-gravity sports or dance in the zero-gravity disco.

Prices for this amazing holiday have been reduced for one week only. (6)

3 **Read the eight sentences carefully. Which part of the text do you think each sentence comes from?**

A The bedrooms are large and comfortable.
B The journey takes about five hours.
C You need a passport.
D See your local travel agent for more information.
E It isn't boring.
F It has the best views in the hotel too.
G There are also activities for our more active guests.
H Would you like a holiday with a difference?

4 **Now read the text again. Choose one sentence to fill each gap. There are two extra sentences.**

Exam help — Learning to learn

Q: What do I do if I'm not sure what the missing sentence is?

A: Complete the other gaps in the exercise first. Then go back to this gap at the end.

Reading

1 **Read these short texts. Where might you see them? Match them to the sentences on the right.** Whole Class

A **Quick and easy photos! You won't find a better camera for this price anywhere!**

B I'm very disappointed with the camera that we bought from you. The box was broken and the camera was scratched.

C When you're looking to buy a new camera, you should compare different makes. Think about what kind of photos you'll be taking.

D If you want to use the flash, press the red button before you take the photo.

1 The writer is giving advice.
2 The writer is giving instructions.
3 The writer is advertising something.
4 The writer is complaining.

2 **Read the article and the questions. For each question, choose A, B, C or D.**

Camden is a part of North London that's famous for its big market. Every weekend, hundreds of people sell all sorts of things, from clothes and crafts to food and flowers. Thousands of people, many of them tourists, go there to look for bargains.

Markets have changed over the years. In the past, you could always 'haggle'. This means that you try to pay less than the price on the price tag. These days, people usually expect to pay the price on the price tag, but some people still try to haggle.

Haggling isn't easy! If you want to haggle at a market, you'll need to remember these things:

1. Be friendly and smile. If the seller likes you, they're more likely to offer you a lower price.
2. It's good to go to the market near the end of the day. Sellers might be tired and may be happier to lower their prices.
3. If you show that you want the item a lot, the seller will notice this and will keep the price high. So hide your feelings!
4. Don't offer a price that's too low. If you do, the seller will be insulted and they won't want to sell you anything.

1 What's the writer trying to do?
- A Describe different markets in London.
- B Complain about Camden market.
- C Advise people on how to buy things for a good price.
- D Advertise the clothes and food at Camden market.

2 What's Camden market?
- A A market in London that's open at the weekend.
- B A famous market that only tourists go to.
- C A market that sells very cheap food.
- D A clothes market that's open every day.

3 What's the writer's opinion about haggling?
- A It's always a bad thing to do.
- B There used to be more haggling at markets than now.
- C It's something that you can only do at Camden market.
- D Haggling isn't difficult.

Exam help — Learning to learn

Q: Will the answer to a question always be in one part of the text?

A: No. In this task, the answers aren't always facts. Sometimes they're about opinions. You'll need to read the whole text carefully to find the answers to these questions.

Reading

1. **Read the title. Predict what you are going to find out in the text.** Whole Class

2. **Quickly read the text and find out.**

The World Children's Parliament

What would you say if you could **1** to some of the world's most important leaders? At the beginning of the year 2000, four hundred children from around the world found out when they **2** the World Children's Parliament. The children discussed the world's problems and they prepared a **3** called the 'Youth Manifesto for the 21st Century'. This was sent to the world's leaders and the world's parliaments.

One of the most important messages in the document was that children **4** to see peace in the world. They were also **5** about the environment and they asked the world's governments to do more to protect the land and oceans. Finally, the document **6** politicians that all children have the right to go to school and to receive an education.

3. **Read the text again and choose the correct word for each space.**

1	A discuss	B communicate	C speak	D argue
2	A consisted	B created	C changed	D grew
3	A document	B email	C postcard	D message
4	A preferred	B loved	C wanted	D liked
5	A worried	B bored	C frightened	D satisfied
6	A remembered	B reminded	C asked	D said

4. **Read the text again. Check that it makes sense.**

5. **Compare your answers with a partner. Try to explain why you chose each word.**

Exam help Learning to learn

Q: How many times do I need to read the text?

A: You need to read it three times.

- First, read the whole text. This will help you understand the general meaning.
- Then read the text again and look at the four possible words for each gap. Try each of the words in the space and choose the one that fits best.
- Finally, read the text a third time and check that the completed text makes sense.

Reading

1 Communicate Quickly read the four texts. Which child is the most adventurous?

The following children are looking for a course to do in the summer holidays. Below are six summer courses for young people. Decide which one would be the most suitable for each child.

1  **Lucy** loves performing and wants to have dance lessons in the holidays. She hasn't danced before and she isn't keen on very modern music.

2  **Joe** is active and would like to try lots of different sports in the summer holidays. However, he can't swim very well and he's afraid of heights.

3  **Gina** is interested in making things. Her favourite activities are painting and sewing, but she'd like to learn a new skill, too.

4  **Chris** is interested in doing some exciting new water sports and having fun. He loves fast activities that make his heart beat faster.

2 Read the information about the summer courses. Choose the best course for each child.

A EXTREME ADVENTURE
This summer course is only for the brave. The action is non-stop and includes go-karting and mountain climbing. There's also a trip to an attraction park where you can ride the fastest rollercoaster in Europe.

B PERFORMING ARTS
Would you like to appear on the stage? Come and learn the skills you need at the performing arts summer school. There are classes in dancing, mime, singing and acting. Don't worry if you're shy, the classes are fun and relaxed.

C WET AND WILD
If you like getting wet, then this summer course is for you. You'll spend every day on the water doing amazing water sports like whitewater rafting, sailing and kayaking. This course is only for children who can swim 50 metres.

D MULTI-SPORTS CAMP
Come and try some exciting activities and sports. There are more than 30 different activities to choose from so you won't be bored. Everyone is welcome!

E COOKERY ACADEMY
Do you want to impress your friends with your cooking skills? Then come along and learn to cook with a top chef. You'll spend the morning in the kitchen and there's an exciting craftwork afternoon programme, too. No experience required.

F TOP DANCE
This course specialises in one of the coolest dance styles around: hip hop. If you love dancing and modern music, don't miss out! There are classes for beginner, intermediate and advanced level dancers, so everyone can learn at their own pace. You need plenty of energy, so be prepared!

3 Check your answers with a partner. Which information in the texts helped you find the answers?

Exam help — Learning to learn

Q: I don't understand it. I've got two possible answers.

A: Don't panic! Read the two answers again. Only one will completely match.

External Exams Syllabus

Unit	Cambridge Exams Practice B1 Preliminary for Schools (Pupil's Book)	Cambridge Exams Practice B1 Preliminary for Schools (Activity Book)	Trinity Exam Practice
1	**Reading Part 1** Task: Three-option multiple-choice	**Listening Part 2** Task: Three-option multiple-choice **Writing Part 2** Task: A story **Speaking Parts 1, 2 and 4**	**Grade 6** Function: Expressing and requesting opinions and impressions Subject: Travel Grammar: Past continuous tense
2	**Reading Part 3** Task: Four-option multiple-choice	**Listening Part 2** Task: Three-option multiple-choice **Writing Part 2** Task: An article **Speaking Parts 1, 3 and 4**	**Grade 5** Function: Expressing Preferences Grammar: Present perfect tense including use with *for, since*; Expressions of preference, eg I prefer, I'd rather
3	**Reading Part 6** Task: Open cloze	**Listening Part 3** Task: Sentence completion **Writing Part 1** Task: An email **Speaking Parts 1, 2 and 4**	**Grade 6** Function: Expressing and requesting opinions and impressions Subject: Health and fitness Grammar: Modals
4	**Reading Part 5** Task: Four-option multiple choice cloze	**Listening Part 1** Task: Three-option multiple choice **Writing Part 2** Task: An article **Speaking Parts 1, 3 and 4**	**Grade 6** Function: Expressing and requesting opinions and impressions
5	**Reading Part 2** Task: Multiple matching	**Listening Part 4** Task: Three-option multiple-choice **Writing Part 1** Task: An email **Speaking Parts 1, 2 and 4**	**Grade 6** Function: Expressing and requesting opinions and impressions
6	**Reading Part 4** Task: Gapped text	**Listening Part 3** Task: Sentence completion **Writing Part 2** Task: A story **Speaking Parts 1, 3 and 4**	**Grade 5** Function: Talking about the future — informing and predicting Grammar: *Will* referring to the future for informing and predicting
7	**Reading Part 3** Task: Four-option multiple choice reading	**Listening Part 2** Task: Three-option multiple choice **Writing Part 2** Task: An article **Speaking Parts 1, 2 and 4**	**Grade 6** Function: Expressing and requesting opinions and impressions Subject: Money Grammar: First conditionals, using *if*
8	**Reading Part 5** Task: Four-option multiple choice cloze	**Listening Part 3** Task: Sentence completion **Writing Part 1** Task: An email **Speaking Parts 1, 3 and 4**	**Grade 6** Function: Expressing and requesting opinions and impressions
9	**Reading Part 2** Task: Multiple matching	**Listening Part 1** Task: Three-option multiple-choice **Writing Part 2** Task: A story **Speaking Parts 1, 2, 3 and 4**	**Grade 6** Function: Describing past actions over a period of time

Unit 1

1 Read and discuss the questions.

Whole Class

1. Have you ever been on a plane?
2. If so, was the plane delayed or did it take off on time?
3. What did you do at the airport?

2 Listen and sing *It's delayed!*

CD4 16

We got to the airport early,
And checked in all our bags.
Our holiday was beginning.
We started to relax.

And then we heard the loudspeaker,
Delay, delay, delay!
Flight 619 to Paris,
It's delayed.

I decided to buy a milkshake,
A comic and a shirt.
We walked around the airport,
Until our feet began to hurt.

Chorus

I suggested playing a board game,
I wanted something to do.
Waiting was getting boring,
I got the airport delay blues!

Chorus

Suddenly we heard a voice say:
'Now it's time to board.'
We were on our way to Paris,
Starting our grand tour.

Unit 3

1 Read and discuss the questions.

Whole Class

1. Have you ever grown any vegetables or fruit? If so, where?
2. What's good about growing your own vegetables or fruit?
3. What vegetables or fruit would you like to grow?

2 Listen and sing *I want to grow some vegetables.*

CD4 18

I want to grow some vegetables,
I want to grow some fruit.
You will be amazed,
As the seeds turn into shoots.
I want to grow some vegetables.
Get your plates ready, please.
Soon you will be eating my tomatoes and my peas!

The first step is to plant the seeds.
They should be in a row.
Then we wait and see
How many shoots begin to grow.

I need to give them water,
And protect them from the snails.
Then I'll watch as peas
And beans crawl upwards on the rails.

And later, in the summer,
I'll take my basket out
And collect up all the vegetables,
That have grown all around.

Chorus

Unit 4

1 Read and discuss the questions.

Whole Class

1 Do you ever have quiz competitions at school? Do you like them?

2 What subjects are you good at? How about your friends?

3 Can you write three quiz questions to ask your partner?

2 Listen and sing *The quiz.*

CD4 20

Who was it sung by?
When was it made?
Where did it happen first?
How is it played?
It's time to start thinking.
My pencil's ready now.
I love doing quizzes.
I love doing quizzes. Do you?

The first round is science.
It's fish and plants and birds.
We work out all the answers.
We write down all the words.

The second round is music.
It's jazz and rock and pop.
We recognise the singer
Before the song has stopped.

The final round is films.
It's actors, quotes and dates.
Our score is our best ever,
We finish in third place!

Chorus

Unit 6

1 Read and discuss the questions.

Whole Class

1 What do you think you'll be in the future? Why?

2 How sure are you? What else might you do?

3 Do you think it's important to know what you want do in the future?

2 Listen and sing *The future is far away.*

CD4 22

Do you think you'll be famous?
Do you think you'll be a star?
Who knows what will happen anyway?
The future is so far away.

I might be an archaeologist,
A politician or a vet.
Or I might be a fisherman,
I haven't decided yet.

I might be a photographer,
Taking photos for the news.
It might be nice to work outside
In theme parks or in zoos.

Chorus

I might be a researcher,
And find important cures.
Or I could work as a tour guide,
Giving brilliant city tours.

I might be a sports star,
An actor or a singer.
But as long as I'm happy,
I will always be a winner!

Chorus

Unit 7

1 Read and discuss the questions.

Whole Class

1 What do you think 'window shopping' means?
2 Have you ever been window shopping?
3 What shops would be good for window shopping?

2 Listen and sing *Window shopping.*

CD4 24

I'm walking down the high street,
An empty wallet in my pocket.
I know it's too expensive,
But I'd love that airblast rocket.

So for now I'm window shopping,
On the outside looking in.
Window shopping, window shopping.

I'm walking past the clothes shop,
I can see a trendy jacket.
If I save my money wisely,
I'll have enough to get it.

Chorus

I'm walking past the music shop.
There's a red guitar that rocks!
If I help around the house,
I'll fill my moneybox.

Chorus

Now it's two months later,
And my wallet's nearly popping!
I'm going to buy my favourite things,
So goodbye to window shopping!

I'm no longer window shopping,
On the outside looking in.
No more window shopping,
No more window shopping.

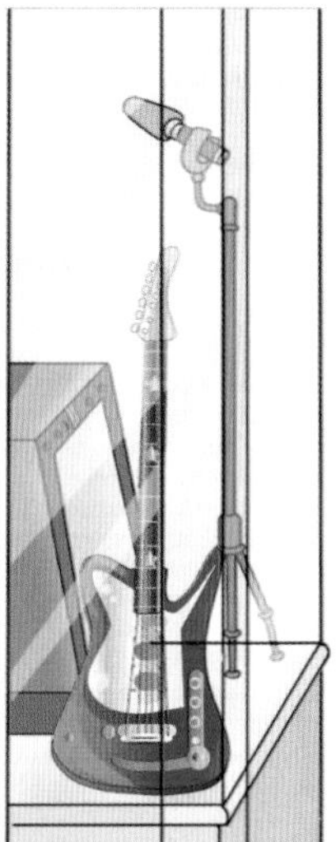

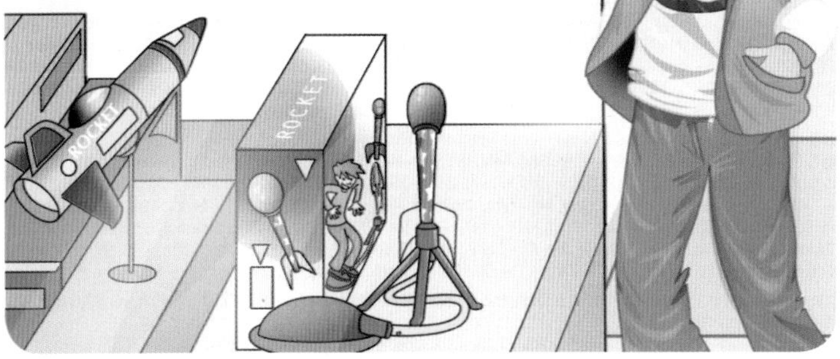

Unit 9

1 Read and discuss the questions.

Whole Class

1 How was life different for your grandparents?
2 Do you enjoy listening to stories about the past?
3 What stories have people in your family told you about the past?

2 Listen and sing *Life was very different.*

CD4 26

I love the first week of the month.
It's the time my granny stays.
We sit on armchairs by the fire.
She talks about the 'good old days'.

And she always says,
Life was very different.
No computers or Internet.
Life was very different.
It was all so simple then.

Her stories of how things used to be,
Keep me listening to the end.
She tells me of the games she played,
And the letters she used to send.

Chorus

She sometimes plays me records
Of her very favourite tunes.
She used to dance with Grandad,
Round and round the living room.

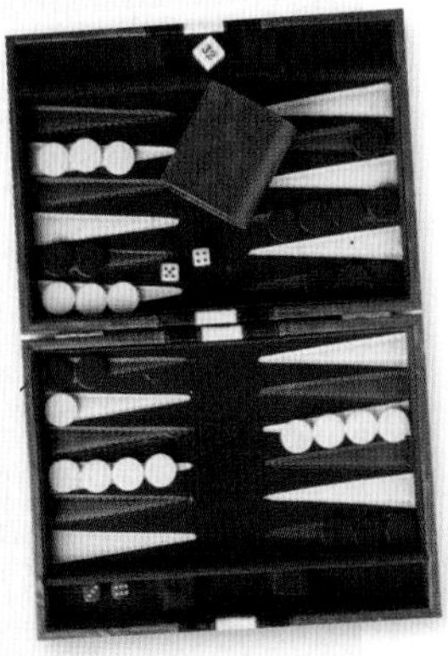

Chorus

She's got hundreds of fading photos
Of old-fashioned bikes with bells.
I wish I could travel back in time,
And see it for myself.

Chorus

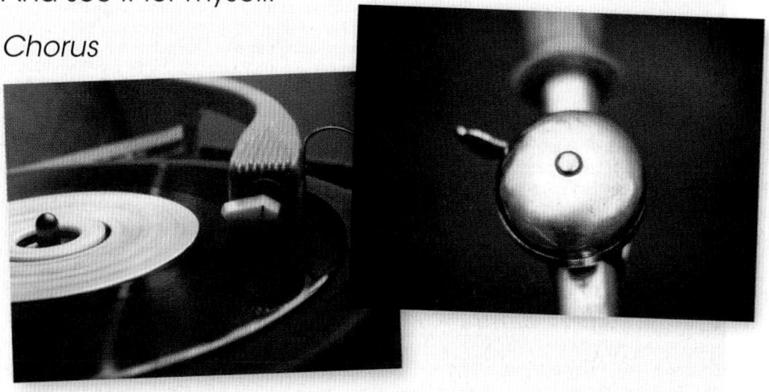

Macmillan Education
4 Crinan Street
London N1 9XW
A division of Springer Nature Ltd

Companies and representatives throughout the world

Pupil's Book ISBN 978-1-380-01361-3
Pupil's Book pack ISBN 978-1-380-01354-5

This edition published 2018
First edition entitled *High Five! English* published 2014 by Springer Nature Ltd

Series concept design by Tom Cole
Page make-up by EMC Design Ltd
Illustrated by Ilias Arahovitis, Leo Campos, Tony De Saulles, Niall Harding, Kevin Hopgood, Sean Parkes, Angeles Peinador, Mike Phillips, Pete Smith, Laszlo Veres, Martyn Cain
Cover design by Bigtop Design Limited
Cover photograph by Getty Images/Uppercut RF/Jules Frazier Photography, Getty Image/Bob Abraham, Getty Images/hadynyah, Macmillan Publishing Ltd/Lisa Payne, Macmillan Publishing Ltd/Tom Dick and Debbie Productions
Picture research: Victoria Gaunt; Fernanda Rocha/Ikonia LLC; Sarah Wells.
Songs produced and arranged by Footsteps and Tom Dick & Debbie Productions
Recordings produced by Tom Dick and Debbie Productions

Authors' acknowledgements
The authors would like to thank everyone at Macmillan who has given help and advice throughout this project. Special thanks from Rob to Belén, Natalia, Xana and Pablo for all their inspiration. Special thanks from Donna to José, Elisa, Teresa and Marina for their encouragement and enthusiasm.

Acknowledgements
The publishers would like to thank the following teachers for their contribution to the project:
Ana Postigo, CEIP Vicálvaro, Madrid; Beatriz García Vaquero, CEIP Mariano José de Larra, Madrid; Damián Quiralte Fresneda, CEIP Claudio Moyano, Madrid; Eamonn Healy, Colegio SEK Santa Isabel, Madrid; Elvira Robledo Gandarias, Colegio Ayalde, Loiu, Vizcaya; Francisco Javier Navarro Pineda, Colegio Tajamar, Madrid; Guiomar Yagüe Martínez, CEIP Celso Emilio Ferreiro, Móstoles, Madrid; Henar Del Gallo Muñoz, CEIP Cantos Altos, Collado Villalba, Madrid; Ignacio de la Puente Rodríguez, CEIP El Cantizal, Las Rozas, Madrid; Inmaculada Romero Fanego, CEIP Príncipes de Asturias, Pozuelo de Alarcón, Madrid; Laura Tenorio, CEIP Esperanza, Madrid; María del Rosario García Leal, CEIP Rufino Blanco, Madrid; Patricia Sanz, CEIP Félix Rodríguez de la Fuente, Coslada, Madrid; Silvia San José Paul, CEIP El Cantizal, Las Rozas, Madrid; Víctor Molinero Cuartango, CEIP Ciudad de Roma, Madrid; Virginia Escalona Monreal, CEIP La Encina, Las Rozas, Madrid; Laura Zarzuelo, Colegio Virgen de la Almudena, Collado Villalba, Madrid; Eugenio Domínguez, Colegio Virgen de la Almudena, Collado Villalba, Madrid; Silvia Díez de Rivera, Colegio Orvalle, Las Rozas, Madrid; Maite Crespo, Colegio Jesús Nazareno, Madrid; Rocío González, Colegio Jesús Nazareno, Madrid; Silvia Valderrama, CEIP Benito Pérez Galdós, Arganda del Rey, Madrid; Lilian Villafuerte, CEIP Rosa Chacel, Collado Villalba, Madrid; Cristina Baeza, CEIP Rosa Chacel, Collado Villalba, Madrid; Carlota Padovani, CEIP Vicálvaro, Madrid; Leyre, Alcalde CEIP Cortes de Cádiz, Madrid; María Andrés, Colegio Matter Inmaculata, Madrid.

The author and publishers would like to thank the following for permission to reproduce their images:
Alamy Stock Photo/ableimages pp73(tr), 112(br), Alamy Stock Photo/AgStock Images, Inc.p31(br), Alamy Stock Photo/Kadir Aktay p27(a), Alamy Stock Photo/Ian Allenden p58(1), Alamy/amana images inc. p113(1-tl), Alamy Stock Photo/Kobryn Andrii p111(2-bl), Alamy Stock Photo/Angela Hampton Picture Library p61(cmr), Alamy Stock Photo/Art Directors & TRIP pp51(11), 110(1-bm), Alamy Stock Photo/Simon Belcher p27(c), Alamy Stock Photo/J.R. Bale pp60(8), 111(1-bcm), Alamy Stock Photo/Andreas Berthold p23(stamps), Alamy Stock Photo/Juniors Bildarchiv GmbH p33(3), Alamy Stock Photo/Blend Images pp16(1), 18(tm), 19(Mei), 20(Mei), 26(Mei), 40(Kenji), 42(Kenji), 48(Kenji), 82(Eva), 83(Eva), 84(Eva), 90(Eva), Alamy Stock Photo/B. O'Kane p26(2), Alamy Stock Photo/BSIP SA pp50(5), 110(1-tcm), Alamy Stock Photo/Classic Image p42(br), Alamy Stock Photo/Thomas Cockrem pp23(needlework), 114(2-tmr), Alamy Stock Video/Ashley Cooper p17(c), Alamy Stock Photo/Cultura Creative p114(1-tmr), Alamy Stock Photo/veryan dale p93(cr), Alamy Stock Photo/Danita Delimont p104(a), Alamy Stock Photo/Design Pics Inc p82(br), Alamy Stock Photo/Andrew Desmond p7(tl), Alamy Stock Photo/D. Hurst pp28(7), 108(1-bml), Alamy Stock Photo/Andre Distel p83(background), Alamy Stock Photo/Lev Dolgachov p68(cl), Alamy Stock Photo/dpa picture alliance archive p95(tr), Alamy Stock Photo/Chad Ehlers p109(1-br), Alamy Stock Photo/Elena Elisseeva pp33(1), 108(2-tl), Alamy Stock Photo/foodfolio p38(tr), Alamy Stock Photo/Fresh Start Images p74(cl), Alamy Stock Photo/fStop Images GmbH p45(8), Alamy Stock Photo/Alex Genovese pp28(5), 108(1-tmc), Alamy Stock Photo/Geo-grafika p29(cr), Alamy Stock Photo/Chris Gibson p7(cr), Alamy Stock Photo/Glowimages RM p112(1-bcl), Alamy Stock Photo/Matt Griggs p41(tl), Alamy Stock Photo/Bob Handelman pp45(1), 109(2-tl), Alamy Stock Photo/Christoph Hermann p78(cm), Alamy Stock Photo/Hero Images Inc. pp8(6), 61(10), 111(1-bl), 106(1-tmr), Alamy Stock Photo/Richard Human p75(br), Alamy Stock Photo/imageBROKER p21(tr), Alamy Stock Photo/Imagesource pp33(4), 34(br), Alamy Stock Photo/ivgalis p30(cl), Alamy Stock Photo/Brian Jackson pp72(6), 112(1-tcr), Alamy Stock Photo/Pete Jenkins p23(cards), Alamy Stock Photo/JG Photography p106(2-br), Alamy Stock Photo/Juice Images p114(2-bml), Alamy Stock Photo/Kuttig - People p108(2-tml), Alamy Stock Photo/Kzenon p104(tcr), Alamy Stock Photo/Michelle Lane pp40(5), 109(1-bm), Alamy Stock Photo/LightField Studios p16(cl), Alamy Stock Photo/Yannick Luthy p41(cr), Alamy Stock Photo/Gunter Marx/SW p82(tr), Alamy Stock Photo/MBI pp93(tm), 97(1C), Alamy Stock Photo/moodboard p97(1B), Alamy Stock Photo/Antony Nettle p106(1-bmr), Alamy Stock Photo/Nikreates p112(1-tcm), Alamy Stock Photo/Roberto Nistri p105(bm), Alamy Stock Photo/OJO Images Ltd p111(2-tl), Alamy Stock Photo/Losevsky Pavel p23(models), Alamy Stock Photo/Photononstop p91(b), Alamy Stock Photo/Photopat p97(2C), Alamy Stock Photo/Isabelle Plasschaert p107(2-br), Alamy Stock Photo/Prisma by Dukas Presseagentur GmbH pp18(9), 107(1-bmr), Alamy Stock Photo/Radharc Images pp8(8), 106(1-bmc), Alamy Stock Photo/Radius Images pp72(Kelvin), 73(Kelvin), 74(Kelvin), 80(Kelvin), Alamy Stock Photo/Simon Rawles p75(tr), Alamy Stock Photo/Simon Reddy p29(cl), Alamy Stock Photo/Mark Richardson pp50(3), 110(1-tr), Alamy Stock Photo/Rtimages p114(1-bl), Alamy Stock Photo/RubberBall pp41(11), 109(1-bl), Alamy Stock Photo/Alex Segre p43(tr), Alamy Stock Photo/Dmitriy Shironosov pp16(cl), 48(cl), 90(cl), Alamy Stock Photo/Stockbroker p107(2-tml), Alamy Stock Photo/Rufus Stone p106(1-tl), Alamy Stock Photo/jeremy sutton-hibbert p63(br), Alamy Stock Photo/Tetra Images pp29(10), 108(1-bl), Alamy Stock Photo/Samo Trebizan p38(cl), Alamy Stock Photo/True Images p80(cl), Alamy Stock Photo/UrbanImages p106(2-ml), Alamy Stock Photo/Wavebreak Media ltd pp61(9), 111(2-tr), 111(1-bcr), Alamy Stock Photo/Finnbarr Webster p16(2), Alamy Stock Photo/WENN Ltd p21(br), Alamy Stock Photo/Edd Westmacott pp51(12), 110(1-br); **BananaStock** p37(br); **Brand X Pictures** pp50(4-trees), 110(1-tcl-trees), 112(1-tr), 127(bm); **Comstock images** p126(br); **Corbis** pp80(4), 113(1-tcm); **Creatas** p113(1-bm); **Digital Vision** pp9(tr), 70(tr), 106(1-bc, 1-br); DigitalVision/PunchStock/Studio 442 pp50(4-bikes), 110(1-tcl-bikes); **©Fairtrade Foundation** p76(logo); **Fancy**/Punchstock/Getty Images p126(tmr); **Getty Images** pp17(br), 18(4), 19(tmr), 29(8, 11, 12), 38(cr), 53(tr), 73(cr), 79, 92(5), 107(1-bc, 1-tml), 108(1-tl, 1-tc, 1-bmc, 1-bc, 1-br), 109(1-tr), 114(1-tmc), 116, Getty Images/Alija p112(1-bcm), Getty Images/AndyL p112(1-bcr), Getty Images/Australian Scenics p105(background), Getty Images/Greg Bajor pp9(9), 106(bmr), Getty Images/Barcin pp18(5), 107(1-tmc), Getty Images/Bart Co p61(cml); Getty Images/axel bernstorff p113(bcr), Getty Images/Bobby Bank p104(tr), Getty Images/Casper Benson pp92(6), 114(1-tmr), Getty Images/axel bernstorff p83(9), Getty Images/BFG Images p100(3), Getty Images/Katarzyna Bialasiewicz p41(9), Getty Images/Matt Bird p9(10), Getty Images/BJI/Blue Jean Images p48(4), Getty Images/Blend Images/Hill Street Studios pp60(4), 111(tr), Getty Images/Blend Images/JGI/Jamie Grill p58(2), Getty Images/Bliznetsov pp61(12), 111(1-br), Getty Images/blue jean images p18(8), Getty Images/bowdenimages p72(br), Getty Images/Brand X Pictures/Blend Images - KidStock pp8(Julie), 10(Julie), 16(Julie), Getty Images/bykac p45(3), Getty Images/Cheryl Chenet p95(bl), Getty Images/Richard Clarkson/EyeEm p91(c), Getty Images/FABRICE COFFRINI p11(cl), Getty Images/claudiodivizia pp72(5), 112(1-tcm), Getty Images/Compassionate Eye Foundation/Robert Kent p100(cl), Getty Images/Compassionate Eye Foundation/Chris Ryan p49(br), Getty Images/Comstock Images/Thinkstock Images p59(br), Getty Images/Tanya Constantine pp45(4), 109(tcr), Getty Images/Corbis p109(1-tcm), Getty Images/Livia Corona p29(cm), Getty Images/CUHRIG p27(d), Getty Images/Robert Daly pp60(2), 111(1-tl), Getty Images/Dave2003 p78(bl), Getty Images/DEA PICTURE LIBRARY p53(cr), Getty Images/Steve Debenport pp98, 108(2-bml), Getty Images/Dianne Avery Photography pp60(tr), 61(Morag), 62(Morag), 68(Morag), Getty Images/DigitalVision/Jetta Productions pp60(1), 111(1-bcl), Getty Images/Kevin Dodge p111(bcm), Getty Images/DreamPictures p45(7), 73(tcr), Getty Images/Echo pp56(cr), 114(2-bl), Getty Images/Jason Edwards p113(1-tr), Getty Images/Christian Ender pp81(a, tr), Getty Images/E+/Izabela Habur p56(bl), Getty Images/E+/vpopovic pp115(top banner)-123(top banner), Getty Images/Exotica.im p109(1-tcr), Getty Images/Tim Flach p105(bl), Getty Images/Food Collection pp29(9), 108(1-bmr), Getty Images/Fotosearch p40(3), Getty Images/fralo p11(tr), Getty Images/fStop Images pp104(br), 106(2-mc), Getty Images/Fuse p19(bcr), Getty Images/Gamma-Rapho/Francis DEMANGE p11(br), Getty Images/GBlakeley p85(tr), Getty Images/John Gollop p114(1-tl), Getty Images/Jeff Gross p10(cl), Getty Images/George Hales p102(tl), Getty Images/Tim Hall pp60(6), 97(2-A), 111(1-tcm), Getty Images/Mike Harrington pp8(5), 106(1-tmc), Getty Images/Hemera Technologies p106(2-bc), Getty Images/Hero Images pp35, 45(2), 61(cr), 92(4), 109(2-tr), Getty Images/hija p127(br), Getty Images/Hill Street Studios p107(2-tr), Getty Images/Hiya Images/Corbis p106(2-bl), Getty Images/Jeff Hunter p82(cl), Getty Images/Kurt Hutton p102(cr), Getty Images/Erik Isakson p93(tr), Getty Images/Steve Hix pp60(5), 111(1-tcl), Getty Images/hoozone p81(b), Getty Images/Ralph Lee Hopkins p84(cl), Getty Images/IMAGEMORE Co, Ltd. p20(cm), Getty Images/Image Source pp50(Youssef), 51(Youssef), 52(Youssef), 60(Youssef), 101(br), 105(tr), 112(bm), 114(2-tml), 125(bl), Getty Images/iStock/Getty Images Plus/MMADIA pp4-5(background), Getty Images/iStockphoto/yang5i p69(br), Getty Images/Jetta Productions p114(1-tr), Getty Images/johavel pp50(1), 110(1-tl), Getty Images/jophil p109(1-bcm), Getty Images/Jovanmandic p59(tr, d), Getty Images/Juice Images/Echo pp18(7), 26(3) 107(gymnastics), Getty Images/Jupiter Images pp72(cr), 111(2-bcr), Getty Images/kali9 p113(1-bcl), Getty Images/Bronek Kaminski p17(tr), Getty Images/Mike Kemp p49(b), Getty Images/kickers p63(tr), Getty Images/KidStock pp28(Gabriela), 29(Gabriela), 30(Gabriela), 36(Gabriela), 107(2-tl), Getty Images/Dorling Kindersley p23(key rings), Getty Images/Dave King p105(br), Getty Images/kisgorcs pp18(12), 107(1-br), Getty Images/Kondor83 p76(tr-background), Getty Images/John Lamb p56(tr), Getty Images/John Lamparski p25, Getty Images/Bruce Laurance pp33(8), 108(2-br), Getty Images/James Lauritz pp8(7), 106(1-bml), Getty Images/leaf p126(tr), Getty Images/leezsnow pp18(1), 107(1-tl), Getty Images/Lesyy p28(cr), Getty Images/John Lund/Paula Zacharias p45(5), Getty Images/Diane Macdonald p12(bl), Getty Images/machdas p17(a), Getty Images/Ryan McVay pp60(3), 111(1-tm), Getty Images/Roger Maeder p81(e), Getty Images/David Malan pp50(2), 110(1-tm), Getty Images/MamiGibbs pp40(2), 109(1-tm), Getty Images/George Marks p92(tr), Getty Images/Oleksandr Marynchenko p80(2), Getty Images/master1305 p107(2-tmr), Getty Images/Roy Mehta p97(2B), Getty Images/Rob Melnychuk p114(2-tl), Getty Images/Michaklootwijk pp18(6), 107(1-tmr), Getty Images/Minden Pictures/Kevin Schafer p83(cr), Getty Images/Lena Mirisola p126(bmr), Getty Images/Cyndi Monaghan p107(2-bmr), Getty Images/Mondadori Portfolio p95(bm), Getty Images/monkeybusinessimages p27(tr), Getty Images/moodboard p23(painter's supplies), 93(tl), Getty Images/Laurence Mouton pp8(1), 125(bm), Getty Images/Matt Moyer p83(cm), Getty Images/Multi-bits p69(tr), Getty Images/Nerthuz pp50(4-pages), 110(1-tcl-pages), Getty Images/Nicolas LE CORRE p11(cr), Getty Images/nikitos77 p31(tr), Getty Images/Hans Neleman p17(b), Getty Images/ogichobanov pp28(6), 108(1-tmr), Getty Images/Oktay Ortakcioglu pp45(6), 109(2-bcr), Getty Images/Dimitri Otis pp50(7), 110(1-bcl), Getty Images/pagadesign p114(1-br), Getty Images/Stephen Pennells p91(tr), Getty Images/PeopleImages p49(d), Getty Images/Pgiam pp8(4), 106(1-tml), Getty Images/Photography taken by Mario Gutiérrez. p17(d), Getty Images/Photoshot p42(bl), Getty Images/pictafolio pp51(9-10), 110(1-bcr), Getty Images/pilotka pp18(3), 107(1-tr), Getty Images/Popperfoto p102(tr), Getty Images/Steve Prezant p107(2-bl), Getty Images/Rawpixel pp8(2), 106(1-tc), Getty Images/ReeldealHD Ltd. p81(d), Getty Images/Rubberball/Nicole Hill p114(tr), Getty Images/Samuray p78(background), Getty Images/Oli Scarff p95(br), Getty Images/Daniel Schoenen p38(tl), Getty Images/Science & Society Picture Library p15, Getty Images/Science Photo Library pp97(1A), 114(1-bmc), Getty Images/Ilan Shacham p37(c), Getty Images/Harry Shepherd/Stringer p103(background), Getty Images/Joseph Sohm p106(2-tl), Getty Images/Paul Souders p83(tr), Getty Images/Steve Sparrow pp33(6), 108(2-bmr), Getty Images/spxChrome p73(bcr), Getty Images/Siri Stafford pp60(8), 111(1-tcr), Getty Images/Pauline St.Denis pp92(Sven), 93(Sven), 94(Sven), 100(Sven), Getty Images/Stockbyte pp40(4), 108(2-tmr), 109(1-tcl), 111(2-br), Getty Images/StockFood p104(b-c), Getty Images/Stringer/CARL DE SOUZA p18(tcr), Getty Images/Adam Taylor p118(tr), Getty Images/Tetra Images pp33(2), 94(cl), 108(2-tr), Getty Images/Tetra Images - Jamie Grill p82(bm), Getty Images/Bob Thomas/Popperfoto p14, Getty Images/Thomas_EyeDesign p33(5), Getty Images/tiler84 pp50, 110(8-camera, 1-camera), Getty Images/track5 p55(cr), Getty Images/Uwe Umstaetter p107(2-bml), Getty Images/Betsie Van Der Meer p112(1-bcl), Getty Images/Klaus Vedfelt pp33(7), 49(tr), 108(2-bl), Getty Images/Terry Vine p110(2-tcl), Getty Images/vladvvm p86(pen), Getty Images/Germán Vogel p41(bcl), Getty Images/Wavebreakmedia Ltd p127(tr), Getty Images/WDStock p55(4-5), Getty Images/Westend61 p61(cl), Getty Images/Colin Weston p16(3), Getty Images/Barry Winiker p106(2-mr); **Glow Images**/Caia Image/Chris Ryan p24(tr); **Greatstock**/Alamy Stock Photo p58(cl); **ImageState** p106(2-tc); **iStockphoto** p27(br), iStockphoto/DGLimages p91(br), iStockphoto/scanrail p48(3); **Macmillan Publishers Ltd.**/Stuart Cox p17(e); **PhotoDisc** pp50(4-harbour), 104(background), 108(1-tml), 110(1-tcl-harbour), 113(1-tcr), PhotoDisc/Getty Images pp36(3), 38(cm), 45(cl), 50(kayak), 61(cl), 70(tl), 106(2-tr), 112(1-tr, 1-tcl), 113(1-bcm), 113(1-br), 114(1-tl), 114(1-tm), 114(1-bml), 127(tmr), PhotoDisc/Getty Images/Anthony Saint James p107(1-bl); **Photoshot**/Blue Jean Images p107(1-bmc); **Photospin** p113(1-tm); **plainpicture**/Hero Images p111(2-bcl); **Purestock**/Punchstock/Getty Images p50(4-kitesurfer); **REX**/Shutterstock/Carlos De Saa/Epa p24(cl), REX/Shutterstock/Dreamworks Animation/Kobal p21(bl), REX/Shutterstock/David Fisher p24(cr); **Shutterstock** p37(b), Shutterstock/Ruth Black p48(1), Shutterstock/cagi p91(a), Shutterstock/ChiccoDodiFC p37(a), Shutterstock/Kobby Dagan p40(6-7-8), Shutterstock/Elnur p69(d), Shutterstock/ESUN7756 p88, Shutterstock/Helen Fields Hotelfoxtrot p101(tr), Shutterstock/Oleg Golovnev p41(br), Shutterstock/Gorodenkoff p90(3), Shutterstock/julianne.hide p41(12), Shutterstock/HQuality p90(2), Shutterstock/Image Source Trading Ltd p26(cl), Shutterstock/I'm Mock-up p67(capsule), Shutterstock/Impact Photography p81(background), Shutterstock/Littlekidmoment p59(a, b), Shutterstock/Minerva Studio p69(c), Shutterstock/Mohd KhairilX p81(c), Shutterstock/Monkey Business Images pp100(2, 4), Shutterstock/Sergey Nivens p39(cr), Shutterstock/Martin Novak pp18(2), 26(1), 107(1-tcm), Shutterstock/oekka.k p90(1), Shutterstock/Thanakorn Prichani p58(3), Shutterstock/Rawpixel p125(br), Shutterstock/Oleksandr Rybitskiy p49(a), Shutterstock/Sabphoto p82(4), 113(tml), Shutterstock/Ljupco Smokovski p126(bm), Shutterstock/SpeedKingz p36(cl), Shutterstock/Stokkete p73(10), Shutterstock/StudioSmart p27(b), Shutterstock/szefei p80(1), Shutterstock/TheStacks p59(c), Shutterstock/VGstockstudio p57, Shutterstock/Tatiana Vorona p104(d), Shutterstock/Undrey p61(11), Shutterstock/Wenpei p50(6); **Stockbyte** Royalty Free Photos p114(2-bmr); **Stockdisc** pp34(bl), 114(1-bm); **Superstock**/age photostock p109(1-bcr), Superstock/PhotoAlto p111(2-tcr); **Up the Resolution** pp31(bl), 108(1-tr); **123RF**/Andrey Armyagov p68(1), 123RF/Kitch Bain p103(br), 123RF/Oleg Beloborodov p100(1), 123RF/bestpixels p69(b), 123RF/BlueOrange Studio pp83(10), 113(1-bl), 123RF/dolgachov pp68(4), 69(d), 123RF/Mike Flippo p101(c), 123RF/PÃ©ter Gudella p91(d), 123RF/Jennifer Huls P36(2), 123RF/hxdbzxy p37(d), 123RF/kzenon p69(a), 123RF/Vladislav Markin p101(d), 123RF/Natalia Merzlyakova p101(b), 123RF/piksel p68(3), 123RF/Gennadiy Poznyakov p80(3), 123RF/rawpixel p48(2), 123RF/scanrail p49(c), 123RF/Dmitriy Shironosov p68(2), 123RF/Siberia p37(tr), 123RF/Anton Starikov p101(a).

Commissioned photographs by Lisa Payne/Macmillan Publishers Ltd;
pp1, 2, 4(bl, br), 5(b), 6, 7(tml, tmr, tr), 8(tr), 9(bl, br), 9(bl, br), 10(Jess), 11(tl), 12(tl), 13, 16(Jess), 18(tl), 19(bl, br, bcr), 20(Callum), 21(tm), 22, 23(b), 26(Callum), 28(tl), 29(bl,br), 30(Tom), 31(tm), 32, 33(b), 36(Tom), 38(b), 39, 40(tl), 41(bl, br), 42(Jess), 43(tm), 44, 45(b), 48(Jess), 49(t, b), 50(tl, 8-tr), 51(bl, br, Callum), 52(Callum, bl, br), 53(tm), 54, 55(b), 58(Callum), 60(tl), 61(bl, br), 62(b, Tom), 63(tl), 64, 65, 67(contents), 68(Tom), 70(b), 71, 72(Jess), 73(b), 74(Jess), 75(Jess), 76, 77(b), 80(Jess), 82(tl), 83(bl, br), 84(Callum), 85(tm), 86, 87, 90(Callum), 92(Tom), 93(bl, br), 94(Tom, br), 95(Tom), 96, 97(b), 100(Tom), 102(br), 103(boy, girl, br), 110(bcm-tr).

Commissioned photographs by Tom Dick and Debbie Productions pp17(t, b), 27(t, b), 37(t, b), 59(t, b), 69(t, b), 81(t, b), 91(t, b), 101(t, b).

Printed and bound in Poland
2018
2